Ann and Amanda

Party time!

Jessica and Leith

Paris

Arles
Avignon
Montpellier
Marseille
St Maximin
Aix en Provence
Nice
Italy

Spain

Ooh La La! A French Romp

Dedication

For Amanda

Ooh La La! A French Romp

Ann Rickard

NEW
HOLLAND

First published in Australia in 2008 by
New Holland Publishers (Australia) Pty Ltd
Sydney • Auckland • London • Cape Town

www.newholland.com.au

1/66 Gibbes Street Chatswood NSW 2067 Australia
218 Lake Road Northcote Auckland New Zealand
86 Edgware Road London W2 2EA United Kingdom
80 McKenzie Street Cape Town 8001 South Africa

 National Library of Australia Cataloguing-in-Publication entry
Author: Rickard, Ann (Ann J)
Title: Ooh la la : a French romp / Ann Rickard.

ISBN: 9781741106701 (hbk.)
            Subjects: Australians--Travel--France.
            Australians--France--Humour.
            Food--Social aspects.
            Food--Anecdotes.
             Food habits--France--Provence.
            Provence (France)--Social life and customs.
            Also Titled: French romp
Dewey Number: 914.490484

Publisher: Fiona Schultz
Publishing Manager: Lliane Clarke
Senior Project Editor: Michael McGrath
Designer: Natasha Hayles
Editor: Victoria Fisher
Proofreader: Rowena Hawksley
Production: Liz Malcolm
Cover Design: Natasha Hayles
Printer: Power Printing Co. China

Acknowledgements

Thank you, Coleen Sheffield and Dave and Carolyn Amos for reading the rough manuscript and helping me polish it.

To Palmira Coimbra Wilkie, thank you for reading the proofs with your sharp eagle eyes.

A warm thank you to Isabella Buke, a lady I have never met but who telephoned me to suggest the *Ooh La La!* title for this book. It suits the story so perfectly yet it is a title I would not have thought of myself.

Fiona, Michael and the New Holland publishing team, thanks for your smart editing and ongoing support.

Thank you to all the tour guests for being the greatest travelling companions on Earth. I won't write your names as I have changed them for this book to protect your privacy, but you know who you are. Not only did you make me feel comfortable as a tour guide, you allowed me to film you and now write about you. What an incredible bunch of people you are. I'll never forget our time spent together.

Thank you, Jessica and Leith for putting your business on hold and disrupting your lives for me. I loved being with you in France.

Thank you to all you readers who contact me through my website to tell me you like me. You have no idea what that means to a writer as she sits alone tapping away at her laptop.

Thank you, Hester, for sharing your Ab Fab apartments with us and for being a dear new friend. You've helped add colour to this book. Thank you to all my new best friends in France who made my time there so memorable.

And Amanda ... you burst into my life so recently yet have made me love you as a cherished sister. Not only did you give me your blessing to write anything I liked about you, you actually encouraged me to make you as 'slutty' (your word) as I liked. Thank you for reading the manuscript, laughing at yourself, and being generous enough not to change a single word. No other writer before me has been so privileged. You are unique and my life is so much better for knowing you. (And you are not slutty, just fabulous.)

Finally, thank you to Geoffrey Rickard, the man who does the housework and cooks the dinner so I can write, and the man without whom, nothing—not one small thing—could I achieve.

Contents

1
How It All Started

It all started with an email from a stranger. A few congratulatory words, a friendly tone and an invitation to 'pop in', should I ever find myself near her place in the South of France.

Living in Australia, it seemed unlikely I would find myself near anybody's place in the South of France, so my first thought was to fire back an email thanking this stranger but regretting my inability to 'pop in'.

Ever since my first book, *The Last Book about Italy*, was published in 2004, I'd received this sort of email from friendly strangers. People who had visited the same places as I had were kind enough to contact me to tell me good things—mostly that my books made them fondly recall their own journeys or made them laugh and had given them the urge to pack their bags and travel.

It's very heartening to find such encouraging messages in your email inbox, and I was proud to have received emails from all over Australia, New Zealand, some from Britain and America, and—I have no idea how this happened—one from Mumbai. And now here was one from France. From someone called Amanda who said she lived a life of '*joie de vivre*-unlimited' in a small village in the South of France. Amanda was not a French person judging from the few paragraphs she wrote.

'I like your sense of humour,' she said. 'Your books made me laugh out loud and reminded me of my time in Italy. I'd love to meet you; if you are ever in the South of France, do pop in.' And then, a PS: 'I'm a woman of a certain age like you, and I am voluptuous like you.'

An invitation from a voluptuous woman of a certain age in the South of France who thought (rightly so) that I was a voluptuous woman of a certain age in Australia, was intriguing and it especially appealed to my husband Geoffrey. Sadly, it was not an invitation likely to be taken up with alacrity. How often did a person find herself in the South of France? And in a position to pop in to a small village she had never heard of?

However, Amanda had given me her website address. I clicked onto it and up came a photo of her posing provocatively in a sun-drenched walled garden by a table, beneath a pergola of flourishing grapevines. She was voluptuous all right. And so was her table. Laid out for lunch for at least ten people, it was loaded with large blue plates and big wine glasses. A yellow vase of wild flowers and candles in glass bowls sat in the centre, and I could almost taste the terrines, pâtés, salads and *baguettes* I knew were waiting nearby to be enjoyed by the fortunate lunch guests.

Amanda, dangerously low of neckline, fearsomely full of bosom and enormously big of hair, looked mighty pleased with herself and her laden lunch table. Her large breasts spilled out of her too-tight black top and one hand rested on a curvy hip. Around her neck was an excessive necklace of silver and leather. Her wide smile said: 'Come and sit at my table and eat with me. Join me in good French food and wine; make my home your home.' To a man, her bountiful cleavage and suggestive pose might have offered invitation of an entirely different nature to that of the culinary kind, but to me it all looked friendly, amusing and welcoming.

'I like the look of this woman,' I told Geoffrey, who quickly agreed, and together we explored Amanda's website. It appeared she was a New Zealander, and yes, definitely *une femme d'un certain âge*, who ten years ago had found her niche in the South of France in the small village of St. Maximin on the border of Provence and Gard. There she lived her days in a state of permanent *joie de vivre*.

She owned a large and imposing 18th-century hillside property comprised of two joined-at-the-hip ivy-covered houses. A sunny terrace ran the length of both houses and looked down over a stone-walled garden where tubs of blazing-red geraniums sat around a large blue swimming pool.

Near the pool was that welcoming table under a vine-covered pergola, a table you just knew had seen countless joyful hours crowded with people. The pictures painted far more than a thousand words—several million of them in fact—and they reeled us right in to southern France.

Amanda, the website told us, was mistress of this beautiful 300-year-old property comprising many bedrooms, grand staircases, wooden beams, stone arches and comforting kitchens. The bedrooms either overlooked the village rooftops to one side or the walled garden to the other. On the upper terrace were arranged large tables, a barbecue, reclining chairs and sun umbrellas. A graceful micocoulier tree spread up from the lower level through a manmade hole in the terrace and gave shade over a smaller terrace leading off one of the houses. The walled garden below was a picture postcard of paved space and garden beds filled with geraniums, petunias and pruned grapevines.

Called Maison de Maîtresse, the Mistress' House, it was a property so compellingly charming, so quintessentially French it made us yearn as we had never before yearned over travel dreams. The website told us Amanda was happy to share her property with holiday-makers on a weekly rental basis and promised them a similar life of *joie de vivre*-unlimited during their stay.

Maison de Maîtresse sat in the centre of St. Maximin, a small village with a population of just 600. It was a charming, tightly clustered village resting on a sunny hillside in the middle of vineyards, olive groves and fields of lavender, poppies and sunflowers. The village enjoyed government protection, which meant the old stone façades on all properties could not be changed, ensuring its permanent charm. It was all heady stuff.

I emailed Amanda back and told her I didn't have plans to be in her region, but that it looked so enchanting, I might put the South of France on my holiday itinerary one day. Usually friendly strangers are forgotten soon after their emails, but it wasn't so with Amanda. Geoffrey and I talked about her often. Her website had made us hanker. That table, her property, the village, her *joie-de-vivre*-unlimited attitude. It all fascinated us. At least it did me. I think it was more her large boobs that fascinated Geoffrey. I could never have guessed our simple email exchange that day would result in Amanda and I forming a friendship as strong as one that had been cemented since childhood. I would have scoffed if anyone had told me then, that because of Amanda, within a year I would be a tour guide in southern France and Provence. But it was so. Me, a travel writer who likes to be led, had become a tour leader responsible for a small group who had never met each other and who had put their full trust and holiday hopes in my inexperienced hands. Looking back, it seems such a short time between first hearing from Amanda to making the change from writer to tour guide. Yet here I now was, just 12 months after that first email, standing by the pool in the walled garden of Maison de Maîtresse with Amanda and Geoffrey, surrounded by eight enthusiastic guests looking expectantly at me. Their trusting faces left no doubt: I was expected to entertain, feed, guide, amuse, delight, teach and generally pamper them for the next couple of weeks.

Geoffrey, who had been lassoed into this adventure to act as mini-van driver, concierge, bag handler, sommelier, treasurer, maintenance man and gentlemanly escort, was just as lacking in guide skills as I was. And neither of us had any French words other than *bonjour* and *merci*.

Amanda, ebullient hostess and warm-hearted woman that she was, also had no tour guide experience. She was capable of throwing a sit-down dinner for 60 people, something she often did, and she was well experienced in putting on a party for 200 or more revellers. But she had never led a tour group before, although she did speak excellent French.

The three of us had promised these eight people a revealing insight to life in rural France. We had painted a glowing picture for them: we would linger for hours over lunches beneath the pergola eating terrines, pâtés and goat cheese salads; we would enjoy cooking demonstrations by local chefs who would show us how to fillet and cook sardines the Provençal way and how to make a perfect *pissaladière.* We would visit a twelfth-century chateau in the village where the flamboyant owners would give us a lesson in *foie gras* making, something done only rarely in France now due to the prohibitive cost of duck and geese livers. A local would take us to the nearby medieval village of Uzès where the Saturday markets were said to be the most lively and abundant in southern France; we would be introduced to local life and quirky characters; we would dine in local, family-run restaurants.

We had promised much. Each day would begin with French lessons over a typical French breakfast of croissants, baguettes, preserves and local apricots and cherries. I would give them travel-writing lessons so that their postcards, emails and journals would sing with lyrical prose. Music would entertain them each night. 'We will look after you, amuse you and take you places,' we had gushed to the eight of them in a flurry of emails during the six months leading up to this day. 'Everything will be done for you; you will not have to think about a thing. All your meals and wine are provided, your transport is included, your every need will be met.'

Oh, we loved our plans. Geoffrey would drive them safely to iconic Provençal towns, renowned walled cities and medieval villages. We would visit Roussillon, Arles, Saintes-Maries-de-la-Mer. We would walk the narrow streets of Avignon, scramble over the castle ruins at Les Baux-de-Provence and take a kayak ride down the Gardon River to picnic on the banks beneath the towering presence of the Pont du Gard. We would spend hours at the market talking to the man who made goat cheese, the woman who made terrines, the farmer who grew asparagus. We would visit wine caves and walk the lavender fields and buy dainty little lavender bags and local honey in quality souvenir shops. It was to be the mother of all tours—led by three people who had never before even taken anyone, other than family members, for a Sunday outing.

An explanation is required as to how an email from Amanda led to me becoming a tour guide. A few months after Amanda's email arrived, I was fortunate enough to win the Australian Travel Writer of the Year, an honour and a stunning surprise seeing as I thought my travel writing was nothing more than frivolous entertainment. More exciting than the handsome glass trophy with my name engraved on it was the prize of two business-class tickets with Air New Zealand to any destination of my choice. Along with four nights accommodation in luxury hotels, it was a humdinger of a prize and I still haven't recovered from the shock of winning it.

'Let's go to Paris immediately and then drive down to the South of France and check out this Amanda woman,' I yelped to Geoffrey after I had waved my trophy at him an excessive number of times. I was high with prize-fever but had the uneasy feeling I might get an apologetic telephone call from the judges to say they'd accidentally given the prize to the wrong writer. And so, within a few weeks, we were sitting up the pointy end of an Air New Zealand plane being handed a glass of bubbles and feeling no sympathy for all the squashed-up people down the back.

We toasted our good fortune all the way to Paris and continued celebrating for four more days in St. Tropez, Nice and Cannes until it was time to go and find Amanda in St. Maximin, a three-hour drive from the Cote d'Azur.

'Arrive on a Saturday morning and we'll go straight to the markets in nearby Uzès,' Amanda had said on email. 'The markets are really worth visiting, so get here early.' She had indicated we were welcome to stay the night with her and that was about as far as our plans and expectations ran. So Geoffrey and I left Cannes in our hired car at six in the morning in the middle of a June summer and drove towards Amanda and, unknown to us then, a new life.

It was obvious Amanda was a flirt. Although I knew nothing of her other than that she was voluptuous, of fairly advanced years and owned a stately property in the South of France where she earned her living by renting it to holiday-makers, I was certain this was a lady who liked sex. Her age—just past 60 if she was a similar age to me—and her shape or standing in the local community were not going to be barriers for her sexual encounters. I was positive of this, even though Amanda and I had not even spoken on the phone. Our only exchanges had been by email and were friendly but formal about our arrangements to meet. No mention had ever been made of her single or otherwise status, but I guessed there would be a few ex-husbands left behind somewhere. I instinctively knew she would be happily single, readily available, and up for anything. And here I was taking my husband towards her. Yet somehow it seemed all right. Whether it was my 40 years of steady marriage to dear Geoffrey, or his inhibited nature, or even his lack of self-knowledge as to what a really good catch he was, I don't know, but I felt safe.

Amanda met us at the front door of Maison de Maîtresse, hurtling out and rushing over to our car as soon as we parked in the tiny village square outside her home. I had never before had so much plump womanhood surge at me. The low-cut top, the long legs, the copious curves, the red lipstick, the chunky necklace, the flashy watch with the word SEXY studded into its face in fake little diamonds—here was Amanda exactly as I expected. Unashamed and unpretentious. Sassy as hell. Welcoming, warm and wonderfully wanton.

'Darlings … welcome, welcome,' she shouted and drew us both into her big half-exposed bosom. And that was it. Instant friendship.

'Get in my car and we'll go straight to the market,' she shouted before we'd even unloaded our bags. 'It is best to get there early, so let's go.'

And so into her silver Renault Mégane convertible we piled, me squeezing into the narrow strip of back seat, Geoffrey legs up around his waist in the front, Amanda's bosom pressing up against the steering wheel.

As she drove us the five minutes into Uzès along a serene country road flanked by flourishing grapevines, she told us how she came to live in St. Maximin.

'I brought my son here ten years ago when he got in with the wrong crowd back home in New Zealand,' she said. 'I wanted to get him away from New Zealand so I put him in boarding school in Aix-en-Provence. My mother was French, I wanted to find my roots. My son and I loved France from the start.

We stayed. My daughter joined us later. She is still here now and she has a daughter. I'm a grandmother but don't tell anyone, especially any of my lovers if you meet them. They don't know my age. My current lover is only 36 years old. I am also part-owner of three apartments next door to Maison de Maîtresse. That's where I put some of my lovers if they arrive more than one at a time. I've got two ex-husbands, by the way, both back in New Zealand. I'm still friends with them both.'

All this information, and before we'd even arrived at the markets. It confirmed my impression and made me laugh out loud.

Uzès was a tangle of traffic on this summer's Saturday morning and it was clear we were not going to find a parking spot.

'I usually get here earlier than this,' Amanda said, searching hopelessly for an empty space. After a couple of fruitless rounds of the busy town we found ourselves back outside the market entrance. 'This will have to do,' she said and pulled the silver convertible to a stop right on a pedestrian crossing. She got out and beckoned us to follow. We hesitated, alarmed. The car completely covered the footpath entry onto the crossing.

'It will be all right there,' she said flippantly and rushed off ahead with her large shopping basket. After a last worried look at the car, we just laughed and followed her determined and ample bottom into the busy markets.

The crowds around the stalls were so thick we had to shuffle and sometimes turn sideways to squeeze our way through. We found ourselves surrounded by produce so colourful and fragrant we began to salivate. The tomatoes here were fatter and redder than any we had encountered before; the lettuce came in more varieties than we'd ever imagined; the asparagus was neatly stacked with tips facing outwards in bunch after inviting bunch. Giant tubs overflowed with black, green and mixed-coloured olives. Corn cobs were being snapped up by indomitable men with concentrated expressions and eager women with baskets larger than Amanda's. Endless varieties of cheeses in great wheels and giant slabs sat beside fat, speckled sausages and moist terrines. As we wound our way through the noisy melée, Amanda kept stopping to greet people.

'Darling!' she cried and threw her arms around each one, thumping them in the back with her basket. 'How are you? Lovely to see you.' Everyone in Uzès that morning was Amanda's friend.

'Let's find my cheese man,' she said over her shoulder to us when she'd released a large man from a particularly effusive hug and moved on. 'The cheese man always gives me something special.'

We shouldered our way past stalls groaning beneath myriad varieties of bread until we reached the cheese man, whereupon Amanda began a great deal of kiss-blowing to him over his giant wheels of brie. He giggled, blushed and pretended to protest.

'*Madam ... s'il vous plaît ... non*,' he attempted but Amanda just blew him another kiss and called him '*chou chou*'. He gave in, giggled again and cut her a large wedge of Roquefort with his compliments. It was the same at the fish stall as Amanda laughed, flirted and encouraged the fishmonger with flattery and endearments and received an extra quarter kilo of mussels on top of her order. Geoffrey and I followed her through the crowds in a haze of admiration and bewilderment watching this siren of flirt perform at each stall.

Then she led us to an outdoor café in the arcaded square, Place aux Herbes, where a table of half-a-dozen women sat drinking coffee and sipping wine in the shade of a large plane tree.

'This is Ann and Geoffrey,' Amanda called to the table by way of introduction and the women all looked and nodded and smiled warmly without surprise, obviously used to Amanda towing strangers in her wake. I did not even ask who they were or how they fitted into Amanda's life, it was all too confusing.

The morning continued in this bustling, puzzling way with more hugs and greetings and market purchases and flirting and air kisses, until Amanda's basket was overflowing with colourful produce and Geoffrey held a couple of baguettes under his arm. I followed them both, struggling with bags of cooked chickens and smoked sausages. We were all a little tired now and Amanda decided it was time we sat down to eat oysters.

'Oysters?' I queried as she bustled her way through the mass of people, their baskets all loaded with fruit and vegetables.

'Yes, oysters,' she called over her shoulder and we pushed our way out of the main market square and across a busy street to a corner bar where dozens of small round tables on the pavement were full of people drinking wine and eating oysters.

Amanda pointed to a cart on the footpath surrounded by a crowd. 'The oysters are a specialty, a Saturday morning thing,' she said, searching for a table and somewhere to rest her bulging basket. 'They sell the oysters from that cart. We can bring them back to the bar and eat them here. You go and get them, I'll order the wine and see if I can get us a table.'

It was glorious confusion into which we were happy to be led. After leaping onto several of the chairs the minute the buttocks of a departee were lifted from them, Amanda organised us with impressive military precision to sit and feast on fat oysters sloshing in salty water inside their shells. She said the wine, Picpoul de Pinet, was local white wine with a herby lemony tang and the perfect match for the oysters. By now, the ladies we had been vaguely introduced to earlier had joined us and there was much table moving, chair shuffling and manoeuvering of overstuffed baskets and bags under tables. Everyone managed to crowd around several of the small tables, some clutching long bunches of errant celery, others cradling bags of red tomatoes on their laps, all of us juggling shopping and oyster shells. And in between all this there were more greetings, more kisses, more hugs from passers-by.

'Do you know everyone in the area?' I asked Amanda, impressed and very happy with the fat oysters and the chilled wine in front of me. She just laughed and nodded; her bosom jiggled along in agreement.

When we arrived back at Maison de Maîtresse and Amanda had shown us her cave apartment underneath the two houses, a place that resembled a high-class bordello (I shall give you a full description later; it might take an entire chapter) she began preparing food.

'But weren't the oysters lunch?' I asked as we both squeezed into her tiny kitchen bumping our bottoms and shoulders on the cupboards and shelves.

'Good heavens, no,' she said and began pulling apart cooked chickens, chopping tomatoes and tossing salad greens in a bowl, all with efficient movements in the tiny space.

Outside in the walled garden a small crowd had gathered: some of the ladies we'd met at the market, a young couple, a man with a child. It was no use asking who they were or where they had suddenly come from, or even why they were here, I wouldn't have understood anyway. It was enough that they all greeted us warmly and planted enthusiastic kisses on our cheeks. They were obviously used to strangers turning up at the property. Within minutes the long table was laden with bowls of salads and plates of chicken, cheeses, strawberries, melons, baguettes, tapenades, and jugs of pink wine. We had been home from the markets less than 15 minutes and here was a seemingly effortless multi-course banquet.

'Is it always like this here?' I asked Amanda when she sat down with us and poured a glass of pale pink wine.

'Yes … I am always inviting people at the last minute,' she said. 'I don't care what my place looks like or if it is untidy. That's not important. It's all about having people around and enjoying it, enjoying the *joie de vivre*-unlimited.' We all drank to that.

The afternoon turned into a gastronomic occasion and made its way into early evening when another wave of visitors arrived.

More cheek-kissing and joyful greetings followed as the garden filled with people of all ages, many of them English-speaking.

Amanda went inside and within five minutes staggered out beneath the weight of a giant elaborately decorated silver punch bowl.

'Beaujolais soup!' came an excited chorus from the people. 'We thought you might make it.'

There was nothing soupy about Amanda's Beaujolais soup. It was a festive mix of Cointreau, Champagne, sugar syrup and lemon juice. She placed the heavy bowl on the table and began ladling the pale liquid into flutes. It was the most delicious drink I'd ever tasted: fizz and sunshine in a glass.

'I call it Beaujolais soup because I first had it in Beaujolais and I got the recipe for it there,' Amanda explained.

More people arrived, more cheeks were kissed, more introductions were made. Twice more the heavy silver bowl was ferried back into Amanda's cave for replenishment and before long, a dozen empty Champagne magnums and an empty bottle of Cointreau sat accusingly by the door. The noise level had risen and the garden was filled with a mix of English and French voices in a variety of accents ranging from the lyrical to the twangy.

After a lengthy and boozy discussion on whether the silver bowl should go back into the cave for a third replenishment, it was agreed it might just be a little excessive so instead, we all staggered a few metres up the cobbled road to the village's only café and ate and drank the rest of the night away in a loud and carefree blur.

In the morning, after we had slept the deep sleep of the full-bellied in a charming apartment next door in the small complex called Absolutely Fabulous, part owned by Amanda and her long-time friend Hester (one of the ladies we had been introduced to at the market, we later found out) we told Amanda we had never met anyone like her before and we loved her already.

As we hugged her goodbye we told her how much we appreciated her generous hospitality; we babbled on about her charming home, her warm friends, the extraordinary social lifestyle they lived here.

'Stay another day,' she said, dismissing our thanks with a toss of her big hair.

'We couldn't, it would be imposing,' we said and shook our heads. It had been wonderful 24 hours and we had been spoilt as never before by someone we had only just met. 'We really must be going,' we insisted but with deep regret in our voices.

Amanda wobbled her bosom at us. 'Nonsense,' she said. 'Stay another day.' She was to say this for another seven heady days until finally, reluctantly, unwillingly, we out-insisted her and packed to take our leave.

As we sat in her garden for one last lunch of spicy sausages and endive salad at the long table beneath the pergola, we looked around the pretty walled garden wistfully and said: 'We'll come back next year. We'll gather some friends, book one of your houses and be your holiday tenants for a week, maybe two.'

Amanda looked thoughtfully at us over the salad bowl. 'Why don't we do a tour and cooking school between us?' she said. 'I've always wanted to hold cooking classes in this property. You get the tour guests from Australia; I'll organise everything at my end. I know lots of chefs who would love to be involved. Geoffrey can be the mini-van driver. It will be an intimate tour of no more than eight people. We'll be fabulous at it. Just fabulous. It will be the best cooking school and tour ever.'

And that's how I went from travel writer to tour leader ... simple, no?

2
Meet the Guests

So, now let me tell you about our eight tour guests, for without them there would be no story to tell.

None of them had met each other, or us, before. They came from all over Australia: two from Western Australia, two from Sydney, two from Melbourne, two from Queensland. They were all members of my small, but much-appreciated, fan club. They liked the sound of this Provence/Gard tour when I wrote about it in my monthly online newsletter shortly after I returned from St. Maximin the previous year. They booked quickly and then made their own way from Australia to France.

I had been emailing each one of them separately for about six months and had formed pictures of them in my mind.

It was only to be expected when organising a tour such as this, where all the guests would be together in the same property for two weeks, eating all meals and taking activities together, that it would attract a certain demographic: the lone travelling woman, probably over 50, single women who loved to travel but were nervous about staying alone in hotels and eating in restaurants by themselves. So I was not surprised when seven women booked.

Our one man was interesting. I had expected a gay man as I had asked him by email if he was single and he had replied, no. It seemed unlikely a wife would allow a husband to take a holiday on his own, but I imagined a gay partner would. I like gay men very much, so I was pleased at the thought of having one join us. He would find us the best shops, give us fashion tips, show us how to decorate an attractive dinner table and eventually end up being one of the girls.

But Ted was no homosexual. He had been happily married for a great number of years and loved to travel. His wife didn't. That she would let him go off alone knowing he would be with seven single women for two weeks either took courage or nonchalance. I wondered if we might find out which.

Ted was in his 60s with plenty of hair and a neat beard. He was well travelled and had spent many years in the navy. This navy training had instilled in him the trait of discipline and love of a well-ironed shirt. Ted was to become our champion ironing man, a self-appointed role that he took on with relish. He had the ironing board set up in the morning and often brought it out for another session in the afternoon. He loved the washing machines as well … but I'm getting ahead of myself … there will be more about Ted's ironing prowess later.

Then there was Eve, petite with a fresh face and cute short haircut that gave her the appearance of someone much younger than her years. Within minutes of our meeting, she told me her husband of 35 years had recently walked out on her. He did it while she was visiting their interstate daughter; when he met her at the airport on her return he gave her the news that he'd moved out.

'I thought we had a happy marriage,' she said to him.

'I'm tired of being married,' he answered her. Then he went to live with someone else in another state.

While Eve was recovering from the shock and grief, she had an offer from a generous, and obviously successful son-in-law, to take her and her daughter on a world trip. Eve had travelled all over Asia, America and much of Europe with them before she left them in Nice to join us.

Next, Margaret, also much younger-looking than her years. Happily divorced and quite adventurous, she was out for a good time. Dark-haired, curvy and attractive, with a vivacious personality, she confessed that, like Amanda, she too liked younger men.

Then there was Shirley, widowed, in her 50s, one daughter still living at home in Sydney. Shirley was to become our softy. Her eyes filled with tears at the mention of anything remotely romantic. Her favourite television show was *Sex and the City* and she would well-up at the thought of Carrie and Mr Big breaking up.

On to Sharon: a curvaceous lady, another widow ... probably in her early 60s. With a couple of lusciously big boobies, she could have easily beaten Amanda in a Best Cleavage Competition, except she would have been horrified at such a thought. Unlike Amanda she didn't deliberately show her bosom off, although it always took centre stage. 'I just can't seem to keep them in,' she would say adjusting her clothes as her boobs fought their way out of the front of every outfit she put on.

Her long and happy marriage ended when her husband died and she now lives happily with another partner. Despite travelling on her own to be with us she said she did not believe in separate holidays. 'Couples should travel together,' she announced as soon as we met. 'But he wanted to go sailing with some friends in the Whitsundays and I wasn't going to sit at home alone.'

We were glad she hadn't.

Joan, another divorcée, was the eldest person in the group at age 72 going on 19. Joan was the first one out of the mini-van and off to explore each day. She was often the last one standing at the end of a long evening. She too had a splendid bosom, not that bosoms have anything to do with this story, I just thought I'd paint you a picture.

Gail was our sweet blonde with a husband and two 20-something sons left at home. Her family was happy for her to go on this trip alone and she had braved her solo way through Europe before she joined us and was happy now to be with a group. 'I nearly starved in Paris because I wouldn't go into a restaurant on my own,' she told us as soon as we met.

And finally Rosa, a woman I imagined from her emails would be my age. Instead, a glamorous young woman arrived, looking more like 20 (she was actually 43) and wearing her designer clothes with great style over her slim figure. Rosa had originally booked the tour with her husband, but had cancelled his place soon after booking. She did not tell us that they had separated just months before. We were to find that out in a rather startling and romantic way ... but I am getting ahead of myself again.

We met all the guests at the designated pick-up point at the Avignon express train station and on the half-hour drive back to St. Maximin everyone was charmed more by Amanda's vivacious personality than the pretty French countryside through which we were driving.

When we arrived at Maison de Maîtresse we assembled in the walled garden where we offered them a glass of Kir Royale, a suitable drink for the occasion, crème de cassis topped with Champagne. Before we showed them to their rooms, I wanted to brief them about the property and give them an outline of what to expect over the next two weeks. And we all needed a drink, especially me. The drive back from Avignon had been interesting. Amanda and I were, at Geoffrey's instruction, to use the full force of our twin personalities to enchant the guests right from the moment of their arrival, while he, a man who had never driven a mini-van before, let alone one packed with people, could concentrate on the roads. The three of us had different responsibilities as tour leaders and Geoffrey was going to ensure we stuck to them.

Geoffrey was very brave to take on the role of driver and although he appeared calm, I could tell he was nervous. It is difficult enough to drive a small car in Europe on the unfamiliar-to-us right-hand side of the road, to read signs, to navigate the many toll booths that pop up with alarming regularity and to squeeze a car down some of the narrow roads, but to drive a large mini-van with eight people depending on you to get them safely and efficiently from place to place is quite a challenge. The van was hired from a friend of Amanda's, a bright turquoise vehicle with a funny hand-brake arrangement on the floor. Each time we pulled up, some tricky footwork had to be performed before the van would actually come to a stop. Geoffrey seemed incapable of finding and then working the elusive brake, and each stop entailed bouts of lively jerking and a bit of kangaroo-hopping before the van settled to a halt.

I am a nervous passenger in Europe and a distracting back-seat driver when it is just Geoffrey and I in a car. In this large and unfamiliar van with eight guests as our responsibility I was beside myself with anxiety before we even left the car park of the Avignon station. The journey back to St. Maximin had been an agony for me. Apart from my loud intakes of breath every time a car came within twenty metres of us and my shrill shrieks of alarm each time we had to enter a roundabout going in the opposite direction to that which we were used to, there were my Tourette's Syndrome-like outbursts. 'Christ, that was close,' just fell out of my mouth whenever a car overtook. Cries of 'Watch out, there's a bloody big truck coming at us!' and 'Jesus, watch where you're going' just exploded involuntarily from my mouth without instruction from my brain.

I alternated these Tourette's outbursts with unbecoming gushing over the guests in a fruitless effort to make them feel welcome. 'You're so much younger than I expected.' 'I love your hair.' 'Are you comfortable?' 'You look so beautiful.' 'Want the air conditioning up?' 'Want it down?' 'Your jacket is divine.' 'Everybody got their seat belts on?' 'Are you too cold?' 'Tell me about your life ... give me every detail.' 'Are you too warm?'

I knew I was being ridiculously nervous and making a very bad first impression but I couldn't stop myself. Amanda was in her element, entertaining the guests with charming anecdotes about her exciting life while simultaneously text messaging one of her lovers. By the time we arrived back at the house I was damp with perspiration.

Earlier Geoffrey and I had assigned bedrooms to all the guests. We had only a short time to do this before we left for the station to pick them up. It was the first time we had actually been inside the two houses. He and I were staying in a delightful self-contained studio at garden level, separated from Amanda's cave apartment by the garage. Both the houses upstairs were occupied with holiday tenants until an hour before our tour started. We had not been in the houses the year before either; we had not known what to expect inside.

There was the very important issue of guessing which guest would be best suited to which house and then to which bedroom.

As soon as we were able to get in, we had rushed up and down the stairs in both houses scurrying in and out of each bedroom, trying to decide who would go on the top floor, who might need a ground-floor room, which of the guests could probably go the entire night without need of a pee and therefore could go in the bedroom that would use the bathroom on the lower level at the bottom of the narrow and dangerously steep staircase in the small house. Oh, the worry of it all. At that stage we knew the age of only one of our guests. Joan had been proud to tell us her age in an email, but the others had not revealed any age information, although we guessed they would all be 50ish. But maybe they weren't. Perhaps they were all in their 80s, even 90s. How could we have assumed? Their ages and fitness levels would have serious bearing on who would have which room.

In a lather of indecision, we had run from the bottom to the top and back again in both houses clutching little yellow sticky notes each with a guest's name on it to stick on doors.

Because all of our guests were single, it meant the big double rooms were going to waste on just one person. And we were one bedroom short which meant two of the guests were going to have to share. I was dreading having to make the decision as to who the two would be.

'We'll put Ted on the top floor of the big house,' I had said, then moved him to the bottom floor but then decided to put him back up on the top again. 'Joan will have to have a room with a bathroom on the same level; she'll definitely have to get up in the night,' Geoffrey had panted as he had passed me on the stairs and then ran into the small house looking for a bedroom and bathroom on the same floor. Back in the big house I'd decided Shirley should go in a room on the middle level even though I didn't know how old she was and whether she would find the steps difficult. The marble staircase in the big house swept grandly up three tall flights and comprised dozens of steps. We must have run up and down 20 times in half an hour, placing yellow stickers on doors and then removing them and sometimes putting them back on their original door.

'God, this is stressful and the guests haven't even arrived yet,' I had shouted to Geoffrey as we ran past each other on the staircase for perhaps the twenty-first time. After a panicky half hour we thought we had chosen the rooms wisely.

Of course, we hadn't.

Ted, it turned out, had an old leg injury that prevented him straightening his left leg fully … and we had put him on the top floor of the big house. I fussed and gushed as I took him upstairs and offered to change his room while at the same time telling him I would then have to change all the other guests around. Ted was a proud man. He said he would not let a few (dozens and dozens … he didn't realise at first how many) steps bother him. And neither they did, even if it meant he had to come down the steps almost on all fours like a spider with four of its legs amputated.

Margaret, who we had on the top floor of the small house with the hazardous staircase, informed us she never had to get up in the night, so she would be safe from the potential danger of a tripping accident down a dark, steep staircase. I was so relieved I wanted to hug her but instead gushed on stupidly about how lucky she was to have a strong bladder. Sharon had a large room on the third floor of the small house with a garden view out of the shuttered window over the pool; she was happy. But then there was Gail and Joan, the two I had randomly chosen to share. Their room was large with a queen-sized bed as well as a single bed, but it was a room furnished for a couple with a child, not for a mature woman who would have to be given the large bed out of respect for her age. However, they both indicated they were happy to share and I left them alone, relieved beyond words.

So with our first hour of the tour over, we left the guests to settle into their rooms and freshen up while Geoffrey and I collapsed on the bed in our little studio and Amanda disappeared into her cave to send another text message to her lover.

I'll pause here to tell you about this particular lover of Amanda's. I'd never met him but I'd seen pictures aplenty of him; Amanda had them scattered all around her bedroom. In most of them he was on her bed naked with a sheet draped modestly over his lower half. At 36 years of age, he looked like a model. His hair was slicked back, his teeth were white and square and he had rock-hard abdominals. He had been Amanda's lover for a couple of years and was single and free at the time they started their relationship. Whenever Amanda felt frisky she would text him. 'Come around right now,

I need sex.' He always turned up on her doorstep within half an hour. Even after he found himself a steady girlfriend the arrangement with Amanda continued, although his visits were reduced to just once a week. Amanda actually preferred that he was settled with a girlfriend; she wanted nothing more from him than sex. Then one calamitous day, the girlfriend spied one of Amanda's text messages and, understandably, the *merde* hit the fan.

'I can come around no more,' he reluctantly told Amanda after the *merde* had settled. 'My girlfriend is a little upset.' Even for a French man used to his woman used to her man having a mistress, this was an understatement. Amanda was disappointed but not too much so because she had since found a new Moroccan lover. At 40, he was just a touch too old for her; however, his Antonio Banderas good looks were compensation, and he had firmer abdominals and other attractions of bigger proportions than the original lover— good reasons to overlook his advanced years. Unfortunately, he lived in Morocco; she had met him while holidaying there.

After a few months of separation from the first lover while he laid low with his girlfriend and waited for the risky situation to settle, and not nearly enough return visits to Morocco, Amanda made a discreet telephone call.

'I want to start seeing you again,' she whispered into the phone to the first lover.

'I want to see you too,' he whispered in reply. 'But I cannot come to your home. Someone might see me. Can you come into the countryside and meet me in my truck.'

He obviously had work that involved him owning a truck—Amanda never explained exactly what and I was so caught up in the thrill of the story I forgot to ask. So now Amanda meets him once a week for sex in the truck in the Provence fields and meets the Moroccan once a month for sex in Fez. She is happy with these arrangements. In between she is constantly alert for any new young blood.

She went for a truck-tryst the day before our guests arrived. It was gloriously sunny and Geoffrey and I had anticipated a day of complete rest before the frantic pace of the next two weeks. But instead of sitting by the pool in the morning, enjoying a long lunch under the pergola followed by an afternoon nap and a leisurely dinner, we had spent the day cleaning.

Amanda had told us the year before she did not bother about the tidiness of her property and although at the time we agreed that a relaxed hostess who gave generous attention to her guests was far more preferable than a hostess worrying over an unswept path, we could not agree with such a philosophy now. We had eight people arriving the next day and all of them had been told in the most effusive terms about the charms of this French property. When we had arrived at Amanda's the day before we were alarmed to have found none of the cushions on the many chairs had been washed since the winter; neither had the many glass candle holders. The garden, charming though it was with its abundant foliage, needed sweeping every day. Amanda thought sweeping once a week was an intrusion on her *joie de vivre* time.

So, while Amanda went off to the country to meet the lover in his truck, Geoffrey weeded the garden beds and I took all the cushions off the chairs and shoved them, half a dozen at a time, into one of the washing machines housed in the garage ... a garage that had not been home to a car for many years due to the extraordinary number of 'treasures' Amanda had collected over the past ten years, including endless boxes of wine glasses, jugs, plates, cups and cutlery. To get into the garage required stepping over crates, buckets, pool cleaning equipment, reclining chairs, bins and old furniture. My efforts to clean it up only resulted in moving boxes from A to B and back again, and when the front-loading washing machine had finished yet another load of cushions and I'd opened it to find three of the cushions had burst and vomited out a mass of bright multi-coloured foam rubber pieces, the garage mess was total. The foam rubber showered everything in the garage and spilled outside into the garden beds.

When Amanda returned from her country tryst, the big smile on her face immediately fell away at the sight of me standing ankle-deep in a pile of pink and blue foam rubber. We spent the rest of the day picking up tiny bits of foam, sewing up the seams of cushions and then removing even more bits of foam from the washing machine.

Then the washing machine, choked with jetsam, finally conked out completely.

Amanda was not happy. She let her anger be known with a stern narrowing of the eyes. I was ashamed, but I wasn't going to let her get away with it.

'Serves you right for going off for a fuck in a truck and leaving me here alone,' I said and then we both fell about laughing.

I was very nervous about this tour. I wanted everyone to love each other and to embrace all the activities we'd planned. Amanda and I might have looked capricious and acted carefree but we had put an enormous amount of planning into this. We had spent countless hours emailing each other, refining and polishing an itinerary of great ambition. The local guest chefs who would demonstrate and cook for us were many and varied and had agreed to be part of this tour because of their fondness for Amanda.

One of them, Dean, a respected New Zealand chef now working in France on a canal boat, agreed to leave his kitchen duties to come to St. Maximin and conduct a cooking class for us. How Amanda met him, let alone convinced him to leave his job and travel a few hundred kilometres just to be with us for one day is something I never found out. I quickly became used to her performing these small miracles.

Maurice, a delightful silver-haired French man and Amanda's friend of 40 years, was bringing his wife Françoise, a home cook of some reputation in Lyon, to stay with us for a week. Françoise would make her famous *coq au vin* and duck-liver soufflé; Maurice would play his piano accordion and conduct the French lessons.

Michel, a stylish gay man from a nearby village who ran a *chambre d'hôte* with his husband (they married in an official ceremony the year before), would also come and cook for us. To give the cooking demonstration some added flamboyance, Michel would wear his pink boa and don his high heels and miniskirt. And if Amanda and I didn't think it was too over-the-top, he would also wear his beloved fish-net tights.

Joanne, an English woman living nearby who ran a catering business said she would theme a dinner for us one night and share her caterer's secrets for easy entertaining. She would also do all the catering for a concert Amanda had organised at Maison de Maîtresse. A New Orleans-style jazz band was visiting the area and Amanda, being Amanda, could not resist booking them for a private concert in her garden. That she now had to sell 90 tickets to cover her costs bothered her not at all.

Word of the Ann and Amanda inaugural tour had spread much further than the village of St. Maximin and down the road into Uzès. News of it had even travelled as far as Spain.

Rosemary, a Spanish chef and old friend of Maurice and Françoise had insisted on joining in. She was prepared to travel to France for two nights to be with us.

'All the way from Spain?' I asked Amanda in disbelief when she told me this exciting news.

'Yes, she wants to be involved in our inaugural tour and cooking school,' she answered. 'She is a brilliant cook. She's going to do a seafood dish for us and other typical Spanish foods.'

I had told our guests all this news earlier when we were in the garden enjoying a second glass of Kir Royale. I had then given them a few housekeeping instructions, told them, as much as I could, how the houses functioned and asked them to keep in mind that this beautiful property we were going to live in for the next two weeks was actually older than the discovery of Australia.

'The plumbing may be a little noisy,' I warned. 'And maybe there will be creaking sounds in the night. It is a magnificent property, a strongly built property 300 years old, but as you can see, it's not a five-star hotel. There is no air-conditioning or room service, no receptionist on the end of a telephone. You are in a beautiful eighteenth-century property and you must accept it for what it is.'

They had all nodded with complete understanding. Then I'd added: 'However, if you have any problem at all, if you are not happy with anything, no matter how insignificant you think it is, come and see us quickly and we will ensure Geoffrey sorts it out immediately.'

When the guests had unpacked and rested, they reconvened in the garden for the Beaujolais soup experience before dinner. They had all changed into fresh outfits. It was extraordinary how quickly they had taken to each other. Extravagant compliments on their appearances were swapped, little exclamations of excitement buzzed between them as they discovered hidden nooks and other charms of the newly swept and weeded gardens. Then Amanda came out wearing what she always wears when she is relaxing around the house. Nothing. Actually she does cover her nakedness with a see-through sarong of a bright lime-green colour tied above her bosom. But that's all.

I had warned our guests, in a gentle and subtle way, about Amanda's outrageous but delightful personality. I had hinted that she was somewhat over-the-top, so now they accepted her semi-nakedness as though this was the way all their dinner hosts dressed and they happily watched her unfettered breasts jiggle beneath the wisp of sheer sarong fabric as she ladled out the Beaujolais soup.

After our first fizzy glass, the guests wanted to see inside Amanda's cave and she didn't hesitate to invite them in.

Her cave apartment directly beneath the small house, La Petite Maison, is tiny, charismatic and quite astonishing. Entry from the walled garden leads right into the bedroom and tiny sitting area where Amanda has crammed enough exotic furniture and *objet d'art* to fill a ten-bedroom mansion. Her large bed with gold-painted headboard and burgundy-patterned bedspread overflows with scarlet and purple cushions. A canopy of burgundy tulle falls from a hook in the stone ceiling in great swathes of exoticness all around the bed. A Moroccan chest encrusted with hundreds of colourful stones and tiny glass shards sits on the floor at the end of the bed. The bedside tables are covered with framed photos, mostly of young attractive men and Amanda drinking wine in various European cities or frolicking on the beaches in Greece, but there are also pictures of her lovely daughter, adorable granddaughter and good-looking son.

A screen separating the bed from the tiny sitting space is barely visible beneath a profusion of boas, scarves and wraps in flamboyant colours. Amongst the mass, a white shawl is the only garment not of a brash hue, although the snowball pom poms dangling from its edges ensure it is in keeping with the gaudy quality of its mates. It all looks like a prop from an old Mae West movie.

A cupboard in the bedroom acts as Amanda's office. To actually get into the office you have to mount a stone step, duck your head beneath a stone arch and then immediately sidle into the chair. A tall person must crouch in there and only one person at a time can fit in. The chair swivels to the computer on one side and around to the other to a piece of flat board that acts as a desk built into an arched alcove. Every centimetre of the stone office walls is covered with photos of Amanda. There are photos of her eating in tiny Parisian cafés with good-looking young men and drinking coffee with swarthy types in moody Moroccan cafés. There are photos of her with frangipanis in her hair and great extravagant pieces of jewellery at her neck; photos of her in the sheer green sarong on the pristine beaches in New Zealand. There are photos everywhere. And calendars. Calendars showing firemen, footballers, surfers and policemen, all semi-naked and provocatively posed.

After the guests had taken turns to squeeze into the office and shriek with a mix of shock and delight at the photos and calendars, they wanted to see more of this extraordinary cave. They queued to file tightly up the couple of stone steps from the bedroom into the tiny kitchen crowded with shelves and paraphernalia.

Behind the kitchen through a low door, Amanda has turned an old storage cupboard into a compact bathroom. As you might imagine, the bathroom is home to several hundred items of beauty products and make-up. On the other side of the kitchen, another low door leads to a narrow staircase which takes you up to the front entry hall of the property at street level. Amanda has turned the bottom half of this staircase into ... ready for it? A pantry! Shelves have been assembled on one side of the staircase and are filled with bottles of olive oil and sea salt, cans of haricot beans and jars of duck fat. To get up the stairs, a person larger or wider than a 10-year-old must turn sideways and do a shimmy past the shelves. Over the next two weeks I found I could never mount these stairs without brushing my belly against jars of pickles and cans of olives.

The guests explored Amanda's cave, crowding around the bed, gasping at the cushions, the tulle, the photos. They examined the boas and shawls and necklaces and some of them tried them on. Even Ted enjoyed it tremendously.

When they at last trooped back out to the garden they were laughing and chatting like old friends. We all gathered around the big silver punch bowl for more Beaujolais soup and to discuss our evening ahead. Françoise had arrived with fresh rabbits and condiments to make her signature dish of rabbit in mustard cream sauce. Her husband Maurice was right behind her with his piano accordion.

So far everything was very good.

3

Filming the Fun

efore I continue with this story and bang on about last night's successful cooking demonstration and dinner, there are a couple of other things I have to tell you.

I can't quite remember how the idea came up, but Amanda and I had decided this French tour would make a good lifestyle television program, a six-part series even: Ann the author and Amanda the flirt muddling their clumsy but charming way through their inaugural tour. The idyllic French countryside would be the perfect backdrop for our whimsical activities and Geoffrey would provide the essential solid character balance for our charismatic personalities. Over many emails we told each other what a splendid premise it was for a colourful lifestyle program. Everyone loved these programs. The pay television channels were saturated with such shows, usually hosted by people far less attractive and outgoing than us. There was a program featuring a most ordinary-looking middle-aged English couple buying a snail farm in Spain. 'A snail farm indeed!' Amanda had snorted when I told her it was currently showing for the second time on Australian television. 'How boring,' she sniffed. Snail farms were obviously horrible slimy things, nothing compared to our glamorous project. Then there was the program featuring the unappealing old gay couple building a villa in Greece. 'I'm over it,' Amanda scoffed. And then, the final insult to Amanda's vision of herself as a television personality, there was the program starring a turbaned Indian man and an uptight English guy renovating a home in France, a region not nearly as beautiful as Amanda's region according to Amanda. She was particularly outraged by this program. If a man can prance about in an unattractive area of France wearing a turban, why couldn't she prance about in a picturesque area wearing a see-through sarong?

The idea grew to become a fixation with her. Why couldn't we have cameras follow us around recording our gorgeous goings-on? We could be filmed buying tomatoes at the Uzès markets, running happily through lavender fields, looking suitably engrossed as we watched cooking demonstrations. How attractive would we look amongst the Provençal grapevines and poppy fields? How glamorous we would be standing in front of châteaux and castles in the medieval towns and villages! How captivating would we come across as we sipped a delicate white wine in an atmospheric wine cave and ate frogs' legs without grimacing? Such a lifestyle show was certain to be snapped up, indeed, fought over, by discerning media moguls all over the world.

Amanda's enthusiasm never waned. Being a lifestyle celebrity was much to her liking and it might even bring forth a batch of potential new lovers. While I had a more sober and realistic approach to it—like how would we even go about securing and paying a film crew, let alone editing and producing hours of film into a professional documentary before trying to sell it—I did rather fancy the idea of a lifestyle show about our tour. I am a fan of the lifestyle program, and I could see the potential of a camera crew following us and recording all the colour of our tour. Amanda had sent me an extra flood of emails as she became more and more excited about the prospect of fame and more convinced she would be the next Catriona Rowntree from *Getaway*, or, at a stretch, a mature Tara Reid from the *Wild On* series. I even believe thoughts of sexy Nigella-style presentations filled her head as she envisaged herself in the cooking classes lasciviously licking a bowl of cream or seductively sucking up spaghetti strands. When it came to annoying practicalities—such as how to get a camera crew willing to pay their own airfares to France and film for us for free; how to secure the services of a director and sound person without actually paying them; how to raise the exorbitant costs required to produce a six-part series without us putting in a cent; how to do musical arrangements and voice-overs without breaching copyright or providing a fee for a professional voice-over person; how to then pitch it to a television company; and, most importantly of all, how to get our guests to agree to being filmed—Amanda had nothing but predictable dismissal.

'You'll work it out, darling,' she chirped in an email. 'We'll be fabulous, just fabulous,'

Geoffrey and I had meetings with professional film people in Australia before we left, people who knew a lot about the many pitfalls of documentary-making and told us what we did not want to hear: we would need an experienced film crew of four or five people using at least three cameras; we would need to capture 12 hours of good film to get just one edited hour that just *might* possibly be good enough to use. Once filmed, it would cost about $50,000 to have it all professionally edited and produced ... and only then could we dare to approach a television station. The bad news went on and depressingly on. We told all this to Amanda who just said: 'You can do it, we'll be fabulous, darling, just fabulous.'

Then Geoffrey came up with the good idea of using our daughter and son-in-law as film-makers. They had two movie cameras; they were good at photography—earning their living under the water on the Great Barrier Reef photographing and filming tourists as they dived and snorkelled. They had been married just a few months and had not yet had a honeymoon. We would treat them to two weeks in France if they would film us for free. Once all the filming was done, we would worry about finding a producer and someone who might like to fund us.

They agreed to come, even though they said two weeks following us around with cameras in France would be no honeymoon at all, in fact quite a difficult assignment, and would we consider giving them a trip to Mykonos after the tour which would be a real honeymoon? We said yes, of course. We like them very much. We even said Amanda, Geoffrey and I would go with them to Mykonos, keeping a suitable distance from them, of course. So it was that Jessica and Leith came with us to France with a big bag of equipment, including a very professional-looking boom microphone with a furry cover on it, purchased especially for the occasion. In terms of expecting a classy documentary from the two of them with us as their bumbling actors, I was not very hopeful. Geoffrey was deeply pessimistic. Amanda was deliriously excited.

I also have to tell you about the wee problem we had with one of the guests, Rosa. Rosa is the one who had originally booked with her husband, the woman I thought was 60-something who turned out to be a very glamorous 40-something with the designer clothes who had separated from her husband. Remember?

Two days before the tour started, Amanda received a telephone from Rosa's husband, Gino, in Australia.

'My wife is joining your tour,' Gino said miserably to Amanda over the phone, explaining who he was. 'She probably hasn't told you that we are separated. I was to come with her but now she is coming on her own. I want to fly over and surprise her. I'm still in love with her. I hope to win her back.'

He said he had made all his travel arrangements and would arrive in France the day after our tour started. Amanda told him, rightly so, that he could not stay with us, but there was a small hotel down the road. She gave him its name and the name of her village with instructions how to get there from Avignon.

This put Amanda in an awkward situation. What to do? Tell him to come to Maison de Maîtresse after he had settled in and make his surprise, or tell him to stay away from our tour group and surprise Rosa on his own ground? Would Rosa be happy to see him? Flattered that he had flown all that way to woo her back? Would she and Gino romantically reconcile and live happily ever after? Or would Rosa be angry that he had disrupted her time alone in France? Amanda asked Geoffrey and I what she should do and we decided it was our duty to tell Rosa that her husband was on his way to France.

We let Rosa settle in and have the first night with her new found friends before we told her the news. The three of us approached her in the morning as she sat sunning herself by the pool. Amanda told her that Gino was flying over to surprise her but now it wouldn't be a surprise because we'd spoilt it, but we felt it had been our duty to spoil it because she was our guest, not Gino, and she was our responsibility and we wanted to make sure she was comfortable about the situation.

We weren't sure of her reaction as we sat by watching her face nervously. She went very quiet, but did not reveal anything. 'He's done this before,' she finally said softly, which intrigued us but we asked no questions.

'I don't know what to do,' she finally murmured. We didn't either. But in reality there was nothing any of us could do. Gino had left Australia and was flying to Provence as we spoke. We agreed to let the situation evolve of its own accord and Amanda, Geoffrey and I left Rosa to her sunbathing with a slight feeling of unease

Let me tell you about Maurice and Françoise. Amanda had met Maurice in Edinburgh in the 1960s when she was a gym teacher and I never did ask Amanda what she was doing in Scotland teaching gymnastics of all things, and how come she met such a gallant French man there and didn't marry him. Maybe he was already married to Françoise at the time; he certainly said that they had been married many years. I was fast becoming used to Amanda's vast and fascinating circle of friends, many of whom she'd had for decades. Maurice is the quintessential French gentleman: tall, slim with a head of thick silver hair and a luscious accent. His English is fluent, he is an academic, a *bon vivant*, a charmer, a musician, a cook and a gentleman. His wife Françoise is voluptuous like Amanda and I. She has an air of the comforter about her. Just one look at her, especially when she dons her apron, and you can tell good things will happen. Unlike her husband Maurice, she does not speak English, although I suspect she could. She just chooses not to.

I could never have anticipated what an excellent enhancement to our tour this charming couple would turn out to be, not that I expected anything from them other than some cooking and musical entertainment. But with Françoise's talented hand in the kitchen and her eagerness to cook for us, she was an indispensable gem. Using Maurice as her kitchen hand, private secretary, sous chef, translator, driver, personal shopper and general factotum, she turned out to be a complete godsend and saved my backside on many occasions. Maurice was just as indispensible. Not only did he do all the prepping for Françoise's many triumphant dishes, he went out early each morning to buy the baguettes, a job that Geoffrey had rostered Amanda and I to do, a job we never did, not even once. As well as his cooking and musical duties, Maurice was on chauffeur duty, driving his car at the head of our little convoy on each of our forays into the countryside. I almost fell upon them both with gratitude for their support every morning when I arose confused, bleary-eyed, sore of head and unable to find anything for breakfast or get any appliance in either of the two houses to work.

I felt disoriented for most of the tour. We all know that feeling of being temporarily lost when we move into a new house or office or stay in a hotel or holiday villa. Trying to locate light switches, working out the microwave and the dishwasher, having no idea where the kettle or toaster are kept is all normal when you are in unfamiliar surroundings. I had that frustrating sense of powerlessness for the entire two weeks of our tour. It never got any better. The dishwashers in both houses, with their many buttons and switches, required a manual translated into English before they could be operated, and who amongst us has ever read a dishwasher or washing machine manual? I'd already broken one of Amanda's washing machines, I didn't want to damage any more appliances. The dishwasher in our studio apartment was actually attached to the oven and located at floor level. To turn it on required the skill of a double-jointed circus performer able to stand on her head. I realise I am whining here—what wuss can't turn on a dishwasher for God's sake?—but when you have eight people waiting for you to feed and entertain them and you are constantly hazy from too much excess the night before, these little routine actions become impossibly difficult tasks.

Last night Françoise had prepared savoury cakes to enjoy with pre-dinner drinks, that is drinks after we'd had the Kir Royales in the garden and after we'd indulged in the Beaujolais soup. I watched her make the cakes in the kitchen in the big house cutting large chunks of creamy brie and dropping them into the batter along with strips of pink prosciutto. This was a kitchen foreign to her and I was quietly pleased to see she was having as much trouble as I had trying to turn the oven on. There was a great deal of discussion between her and Maurice over the oven knob. Heated words and cries of *merde* filled the kitchen as Maurice raised his eyebrows, arms and hands to both Françoise and the ceiling.

To add to the confusion, another woman had arrived, a friend of theirs called Luce who was not shy about putting in her bit about the oven and other culinary matters. Their three heads were to be bent over the oven for the next week and I thoroughly enjoyed their vigorous discussions even though the only word I understood was *merde*. I had no idea how Luce fitted into the picture, indeed if she had any role in any picture at all, but I liked her instantly. Like Françoise she had that dependable look about her and she did not hesitate to put on an apron and join in the kitchen confusion. As I was to find out over the next two weeks, French people rarely venture out alone, they always require an entourage. Whenever we were expecting one chef to come in and cook, at least three people turned up, often more. Not once did a chef arrive on his own, apart from the New Zealander, Dean. I never asked who the people were that formed these entourages, or why indeed had they come along at all. I just accepted that they joined in and I greeted them as though they were my best friends. Luce spent a lot of time in the kitchen, hands on hips, baseball cap on her head, offering loud opinions about the oven, and Françoise was not always pleased. Their conversations ran fast and vigorous. *Non, non, non! Mon dieu! Merde!* and so it would go until at last ... *voilà!* ... the oven light came on and everyone laughed and opened a bottle of wine.

When Françoise brought out little squares of delicious savoury cakes to us on the terrace everyone nibbled and applauded her culinary prowess. By that stage it was getting late, but still light; the wine bottles had been passed around the table a number of times. When the rabbit dish came out, carried by Françoise, with Luce and Maurice in attendance, we were all boozily passionate about everything French. As Françoise stood at the table dishing out the creamy rabbit with gnocchi to eager hands, there were cheers and loud claps. She was treated as though she was France's most celebrated Michelin-starred chef who had just cooked a banquet for the royal family of Monaco. She just smiled modestly and encouraged everyone to eat and then partake of second helpings.

After dinner, several more people arrived at Maison de Maîtresse with wine bottles, including Hester, Amanda's friend and neighbour, another New Zealander. Hester had joined Amanda in France several years ago and found a fourteenth-century property next door to Maison de Maîtresse in need of renovation. She and Amanda bought the property together and renovated it into three attractive apartments.

Like Amanda, Hester is single, of a similar age, and lives for much of the year in France in one of her apartments and holiday-lets the others, mostly to New Zealanders.

Hester is chalk to Amanda's cheese. With pale blonde curly hair, a young girl's slim figure, she possesses an infinite chic, an aura of serenity. Her clothes look as though they have all been purchased in Paris. She does not own a see-through sarong. She and Amanda may be opposites but they have a solid friendship and excellent business relationship.

Shortly after Hester arrived last night, another couple came in with a good-looking Irish man, apparently a soap opera actor in his own country. Charm, along with several litres of red wine, oozed from his every pore. His turn of phrase was as quaint as his manners. 'How would you be this grand evening?' he said to each of our guests as he kissed their hands. When they told him they were very well indeed, he replied: 'That's sound, just sound.' What an Irish soap actor was doing in a tiny village in the French countryside was never explained, nor was his presence at Maison de Maîtresse. He was just one of many interesting people to suddenly appear without invitation or warning, but who was welcomed with warmth.

Our other Irish element and the last thing I have to tell you before we move on with this story (I promise) and actually get out and start to tour, is our kitchenhand. Amanda had employed an attractive young Irish student, Ciara, to be our helper for the duration of the tour. Her job was to lay the table for each meal, serve us, clear the table and clean up. She was to be paid well for her cleaning duties, something Amanda and I originally said we would do ourselves but Geoffrey wisely suggested we would not.

'You two do dishes at midnight after you have entertained the guests and consumed a barrel of wine each?' he said, in a caring but astonished manner. 'You will not be even able to clear up after yourselves, let alone our guests. We are definitely hiring someone and paying them out of our budget. It is imperative.'

And so Amanda hired Ciara, as Irish as a glass of Guinness, and keen to earn some money. She is tall and slim, another one with great breasts. She has been living in France for some years and her French is fluent. Like the Irish soap actor, she vibrates charm and uses endearing Irish expressions. Her only downside is, she likes to party, she wants to be one of the guests, sit with us, eat with us, and, as we were to find out to our amusement and consternation, she is fond of a drink.

Our first night had been an outstanding success, the rabbit with mustard cream sauce a triumph, the savoury cakes a celebration.

Maurice sang and played the accordion until two in the morning; Luce put on a little one-woman play in Shakespearean manner about a woman whose husband goes out one night for cigarettes and never returns. Although we didn't understand a word she moaned, she had no English at all, we understood the fake drunken gestures, the falling about, the chest thumping and loud sobbing as she called to her husband to hurry up and make his purchase and return home. Finally, around two-thirty in the morning, our guests staggered off to their beds, leaving the Irish actor and the Irish kitchen hand to knock off another couple of litres of our wine.

Geoffrey and I fell into our bed in our studio apartment and awoke in a lather of guilt and perplexity. We were supposed to have arisen well before the guests, driven to the local *boulangerie* for the baguettes and croissants, had the table set for breakfast and the croissants in the oven. Instead, the guests were all up, showered, dressed and waiting patiently for their breakfast and their promised French lesson.

'Turn the oven on,' I shouted at Geoffrey as he pulled on his pants and I threw on a T-shirt. Geoffrey had not yet mastered the oven himself but I knew he would be better than me at attempting it this morning. I raced off to find cups, saucers, plates and other breakfast accoutrements. There was no sign of Amanda. I was angry with myself for letting our guests down on only the second day, although no-one seemed in the least concerned; they were all sitting on the upper terrace in the sunshine discussing the antics of the night before and gossiping about the Irish soap star.

Ted, who was showing the first signs of turning into Martha Stewart, was busy in the kitchen with a tea towel stuck into his shorts, hunting for yogurt, strawberries, jams and coffee. He had found out where the plates were kept, where the butter lived, where the tea bags were stored and, oh, the relief of it, he had worked out how to turn on the oven. I could have kissed him all over his bearded face.

'Get the croissants in the oven,' I ordered him kindly and, like a good naval person, he set to the task.

Amanda had still not surfaced. Geoffrey was looking very hung-over with his cap askew; I had red eyes, an aching head, bare feet and my T-shirt on inside out. I kept running from the big house to the little house, down to our studio and then to Amanda's cave in the hope of doing something, anything, useful, whether it be getting Amanda out of bed, clearing my head or helping Ted with the croissants. Despite his headache Geoffrey set about cutting up melons and making tea.

By the time Amanda appeared, red-eyed and dishevelled in her green sarong, there was a distinct smell of burning in the kitchen.

Thank God, Maurice had bought half-a-dozen fresh baguettes, and the guests busied themselves slicing and buttering bread, helping themselves to fruit and yogurt, while politely ignoring the smoke billowing from the oven.

Amanda stood in the middle of the kitchen and surveyed the scene. Maurice, handsome and ready at his makeshift white board, the guests munching on fresh bread and biting into big red strawberries with their eyes averted from a nearby tray of blackened croissants, me with my inside-out T-shirt and frantic expression. She gave her sarong a strong tug to cover one of her boobs on the verge of popping out and announced: 'You must all get your own breakfast in future.'

The guests all looked up happily at her. 'We guessed that might happen,' someone said not unkindly, before I slunk off in deep embarrassment.

4

French Lessons

Maurice looked very French in his striped sweater, his glasses on, a blue felt pen in hand as he stood at the white board. This would be no schoolboy French lesson; he was going to teach us properly, concentrating on grammar, on the masculine and the feminine, the past and present tenses. It was not easy for him to hold our attention. There was more laughter than learning but everybody seemed to enjoy it. We sat for an hour and a half in the morning sunshine and although Maurice wrote prolifically on the white board and questioned us on our tenses, and some of the group wrote in their books, there seemed to be no grasp of the basics of French by the end of the lesson. However, it didn't seem to matter at all.

After a muddled rounding-up of the guests we piled into the mini-van, watched Geoffrey struggle with the misbehaving brake, and then set off through the green countryside to the nearby flea market. This was the first of our planned excursions and a small one as we wanted to ease the group gently into trips.

The Sunday flea markets are popular all over France and this local one was five minutes away, an easy enough trip for everyone after the big night before and one that would allow Geoffrey to slip into greater confidence at being the driver for eight expectant tour guests.

My first thought on entering the dusty and crowded flea market was: 'My God, has every person in France cleaned out his attic and brought all his old crap here?' The place was packed with vans spilling out junk; all over the ground people had spread mats and laid out their life's collection of accumulated useless items. Personally I am not fond of flea markets. Looking at my own garage full of crap is unnerving enough, I do not want to visit places where I have to look at other people's crap. But the old maxim 'one man's trash is another man's treasure' really is correct, and let us not forget, this was French crap, certain to be crap of an entirely superior nature.

Within minutes, the group started showing real interest. Someone pounced upon a plate painted in the Aboriginal-dot style. We all laughed. An Aboriginal artefact in the middle of rural France? What next? Actually there was plenty next. As we picked our way through the piles, stepping over old car parts, odd pieces of cutlery, worn wooden bowls, broken children's toys, chipped cups, odd china plates and antiquated brown teapots, Sharon came across an old-fashioned stole, a thing that goes around a woman's shoulders to keep her warm, like a pashmina only furry. It had obviously been worn around the shoulders of a refined French lady who went to grand balls and fancy dinners in the 1940s or 1950s and smelt very old. It was a small black thing, but when Sharon put it on her shapely shoulders it looked most fetching. We all took turns trying it on and I suddenly realised there is a lot of fun to be had at a flea market when you are part of a group. After the stole had done the rounds of all our shoulders including Ted's, Sharon found a matching fur hat in the French beret style. We all then tried on the hat, and Sharon decided, old and ratty though these garments were, at ten euros the two, she would buy them. That she would probably never wear them did not matter at all, it was the memory they would give her when she later pulled them out of her junk box at home that was important.

Within minutes Shirley, our lady who can be brought to tears over a particularly glamorous dress Carrie wore in a *Sex and the City* episode, had found some exquisite linen and lace. 'Look at this beautiful work,' she said as her eyes became dewy. She picked up place mats and towels, all hand-embroidered and of immaculate workmanship. Her moist eyes were wide with pleasure and we all made gushing noises and pretended we loved linen and lace as much as she did. Shirley bought several items and declared her love for every piece of linen and lace made in France and we all felt good about her happiness.

Maurice had come to the flea market with us to translate and bargain, and his reassuring presence was welcome. It wasn't long before each of our guests had grabbed his arm and led him towards a stall for assistance. Gail had spied an old medal and as one of her sons back home in Melbourne was an avid collector, she was in the mood to do serious business. With Maurice as her guide and translator she negotiated a very good price.

I was happily astounded that our guests would actually buy anything at all, let alone find little treasures that gave them so much genuine excitement. I was particularly pleased for Gail and her purchase as we had encountered a small but potentially awful problem with her and Joan earlier this morning once we had cleared away the burnt croissants and Ted had worked out how to turn on the dishwasher.

Joan had pulled me aside and whispered that Gail was not happy about the room sharing and neither was she. Although they had a particularly large and airy room with plenty of separate sitting space, Gail had graciously given Joan the large bed and taken the smaller single bed where she spent an uncomfortable night.

Although Joan did not say it, it was obvious they both felt I had unfairly singled them out to share. Even though I hadn't—the choice had been purely random—it was understandable that they should feel I had not been impartial. The others were all luxuriating in large rooms with double beds to themselves. Joan and Gail had been forced together. How could they not feel cheated? It really came back to our inexperience as tour operators. We should have stipulated firmly right at the beginning that twin sharing would occur unless single supplements were applied. We were very naïve tour operators.

That two of our guests should be so unhappy after their first day filled me with terrible anguish. I immediately passed on this terrible anguish to Geoffrey, and for good measure, also shared it with Amanda. We agreed we had to repair this potentially unpleasant situation immediately so Geoffrey and I offered Gail our studio apartment. This was all done discreetly. I didn't want to cause her and Joan any further upset and I managed to get Gail into a quiet spot and tell her she must move without delay into the self-contained studio with large bed, kitchenette and ensuite bathroom. I assured her Geoffrey and I would find somewhere else to sleep. I was happy to do this. It did not matter if I had to go and sleep outside in the tiny village square on a bench, Gail and Joan had to be as happy as the others with their rooms, otherwise I could not continue functioning adequately for the rest of tour. And yes, I am a considerate and kind tour leader and yes, you can think good thoughts about me. Gail had been reluctant to have us move out of the studio on her behalf, but we insisted. She had packed her bags and we had packed ours. There was only one room left in either of the houses and that was a tiny box bunk room at the very top of the big house opposite the landing where Ted was enjoying oodles of space to himself, sprawling out in a large and light room, complete with king-size bed and separate lounge area with table, chairs and welcoming armchair.

The plan had been for Jessica and Leith (our voluntary film crew, keeping up?) to use the bunk room; they had so far been staying in luxury in one of Hester's apartments next door at Ab Fab which was now needed to accommodate more of the chefs coming to cook for us (omigod, the arranging of it all) and so Jessica and Leith were told they'd now have to sleep on the floor in the living room of the big house, and Geoffrey and I would sleep in the bunks.

Now, at the flea market Gail had bought a medal and all memory of her night in the single bed in the shared room was forgotten. She was laughing and happy and so was I, even if it meant I would (a) have to struggle to climb up old-lady-style to a top bunk and sleep in a narrow child's bed for the next two weeks, or (b) I would have to bend over double and squeeze myself into a bottom bunk and sleep in a narrow child's bed for the next two weeks, and (c) face the very real danger of big Geoffrey performing a particularly vigorous turn in the night, snapping the thin slats separating us, and crashing down on me. I didn't want to think of any of those unpleasant scenarios just yet, I was enjoying myself now with the others at the flea market. We had come across a man with a ferret on a lead.

This probably doesn't sound appealing to you sitting at home in your lounge-room or propped up in your warm bed reading this, but a ferret on a lead can be quite an attraction when you are holidaying in a foreign country. So we all crowded around and watched the little creature scurrying about on the dusty ground. Its owner was a jolly, loud man who babbled happily to us, something about not letting the ferret run up our skirts I think, and it all proved too tempting for Margaret who picked the ferret up and cuddled it. It nestled into her shoulder and we all stroked it and felt simultaneously brave and stupid for becoming so excited over a French ferret.

Amanda had disappeared at this stage and I left the gang with the ferret to go in search of her. Amanda is never hard to find in a crowd; she is always wearing something brightly coloured and stand-outish. Today, she had on a low-cut, tight green top and a flowing gypsy skirt with one of her favourite accessories, a wide leather, silver-studded belt, the kind burly bikies wear. I found her immediately, flirting with a stall owner and contemplating buying a giant frying pan.

'What on earth do you want with that?' I asked her. She already had an exceptionally large amount of kitchenware stuffed into her tiny kitchen.

'I love it,' she said. 'I'll find a use for it.'

'But you already have about 100 frying pans.'

'Well, I want another one,' she said and immediately bought it.

The size of an old-fashioned dustbin lid and weighing almost as much as she did, it was quite the burden to carry around the market so we decided it was time to go home.

We'd had an entertaining morning and everyone but me had made a purchase that pleased them immensely.

We still had the small niggle of Rosa's husband due to arrive tomorrow, although Rosa herself did not seem in the least perturbed. She appeared calm and looked beautiful. Her long, dark hair was so glossy it should have been in a shampoo commercial; her lovely shaped face was serene and relaxed. By now the others in the group had learnt of the love tangle and were intrigued, looking forward to developments whether they were of a romantic kind or of the angry clash sort. Amanda and I were fascinated ourselves. We were very curious as to what Gino would look like. We were certain he would be tall, gentle and passionate ... and dark and handsome of course. He was, after all, a man performing one of the grandest romantic gestures of them all: an ardent dash across the world to try to win back his sweetheart. Geoffrey, typically, was concerned about the outcome, worried that Rosa's two weeks would be spoilt.

We decided it was too stressful to contemplate now and turned our thoughts instead to the more pleasing matters of food and wine.

Our lunch today was to be taken under the pergola in the walled garden. Amanda was going to demonstrate and cook one of her Provençal specialties. Amanda is an excellent cook. She owned a restaurant in her home town of Auckland in New Zealand and her years and experience in the hospitality industry were obvious as she explained the meal.

'I'm going to make little goat cheese parcels,' she told the group who looked at her fondly. 'I toast some pine nuts and place them on top of the little rounds of goat cheese and then splash them with olive oil, top them with a sprig of thyme, wrap them up in foil and cook them for about 15 minutes on the covered barbecue. The goat cheese melts and becomes all gooey, the thyme adds flavour and the pine nuts give an interesting crunchy texture.' This was a dish Amanda had cooked countless times, and with a fresh green salad, followed by the ubiquitous French cheese plate and endless chunks of crusty baguette, it made for a simple but delicious Provençal lunch. Amanda and I had planned this meal long ago, determined to give our guests as much local produce and typical regional dishes as possible.

Jessica and Leith followed Amanda's preparation with the cameras and she explained step by step as she prepared the dish, relishing her role as a celebrity chef, although she did not attempt a Nigella swoon over the little goat cheese rounds.

The guests all sat down at the long table and poured wine. Geoffrey, our wine provider, had already made half- a-dozen trips to the local wine cave to keep up with demand. Our carefully worded itinerary for the guests had stated clearly that wine would be served with meals. In reality, wine was being taken all times of the day and evening. There was no greed in it, the atmosphere at Maison de Maîtresse was so relaxed, so intimate and happy, everyone felt as though they were in their own home. And we liked that, even if it meant dear Geoffrey had to constantly rev the van up, deal with the funny foot brake and make yet another trip down the road for more wine supplies. Our local wine cave provided excellent red, white and our favourite rosé wine.

These wine caves, pronounced 'carves,' can be found everywhere in rural France, charming places ranging from the humble to the grand, where the farmers and winemakers sell their own wine to anyone who comes in. The idea is to turn up with your empty container and fill it from a large barrel or stainless steel vat with a pump, much the same as a petrol pump and indeed, the act is much like that of filling up your car. The wines are so drinkable and inexpensive, it seems mandatory to drink as much as you want. We had allowed for five litres a day. We were drinking at least treble that.

The guests had all kindly been agreeable to being filmed and by now, just day two, they were very relaxed and natural in front of the cameras. We had filmed them at the flea market cuddling the ferret and buying the medal and now we were filming them sitting at the lunch table waiting for their goat cheese parcels and eating slices of sweet melon that Françoise had cut up and brought out.

'Why does produce taste so much better in France?' someone said. It was agreed, this was the sweetest and most flavoursome melon any of us had ever tasted. A lengthy discussion followed on the merits of French fruit and vegetables over some tasteless produce from other countries. We had already bought cherries and apricots by the side of the road and never tasted anything as full-flavoured. Now we all tucked into the sweet melon and drank rosé, and the atmosphere once again became quite boozy.

Nobody, including Amanda, gave thought to the little goat cheese parcels on the barbecue. About 40 minutes later when Geoffrey returned from the cave on a wine-replenishment trip and politely inquired as to the progress of the goat cheese parcels, we suddenly remembered and made a dash for the barbecue. They were, of course, beyond the melting stage Amanda had told us would take us to a gustatory heaven we had never yet visited, and were more like parcels of runny cream dotted with blackened pine nuts.

Fortunately, nobody could have cared less about the runniness of goat cheese and there was a chorus of: 'Bring them on, we'll love them' from everyone at the table. And surprise, we actually did love them. The bottoms of the cheese rounds had burnt to a crispy texture and could be easily peeled off the foil. We tipped the runny cheese on to our salad greens and topped it with the crust and it was so fragrant and delicious Amanda declared she might in future always cook them for 40 minutes rather than the required 15.

We ate and drank and talked and laughed for several hours in the dappled sunshine and continuously clinked our wine glasses in toast of another successful day.

Although it was almost four in the afternoon before we finished lunch there were still many hours of daylight left and everyone took the chance for a rest by the pool, except for Ted who had washing and ironing in mind. While Amanda spread her tanned and topless body on a reclining chair, and our kitchenhand Ciara, decided it would be a good idea to also take her top off and lie out in the sun with the guests, Ted invited everyone to bring out their dirty washing and let him attend to it. As we were down to just one machine now, Ted set about the task of not only learning how to work the good machine, but of repairing the damaged one.

As he picked bits of wet foam from the broken machine, he loudly asked: 'Who in their right mind would put cushions in a washing machine?' and then answered himself: 'Only a lunatic.'

When I confessed: 'Actually that lunatic was me,' he didn't blink or even look embarrassed. He was so annoyed with the machine he decided to pull it apart and have a proper go at fixing it. When its innards were out and laid on the floor, he found bits of twigs and bunches of soggy leaves amongst the mass of foam rubber.

'Look at this,' he announced to the ladies around the pool as he brandished a handful of leaves, twigs and foam rubber. They were, quite understandably, not in the least interested in washing machine flotsam and ignored him. However, the broken washing machine appeared to be giving Ted no end of pleasure and he busied himself with it for the rest of the afternoon in between hanging out washing on the line outside the walled garden. When he discovered the ironing board, also housed in the garage, could actually be brought out to a power point in the garden where he could iron in the sunshine, he became a very content man.

Later, as he brought the washing in off the line and began sorting it, I stood and watched, amazed that members of this group who had known each other for only 48 hours were comfortable putting their intimates in the same washing machine and having a man so new to their acquaintance sort them out. However, it was actually quite wholesome, very family-like and even though the women said they would do their own washing in future, we were all happy that afternoon.

Geoffrey and I heaved our luggage up the three steep flights of stairs to the bunk room on the top floor. About the size of a small bathroom, the room contained the bunk beds, a chest of drawers, a rack on wheels to hang clothes and an enormous stuffed Mickey Mouse as big as a man. We looked miserably around the tiny space. The only thing in its favour was the glorious view from the small window out over the village rooftops to the church spire.

'I can't sleep on the top bunk; I'll never be able to climb up and down in the night when I need to pee,' I complained to Geoffrey who stood by the door as there wasn't enough space for him to fit in the room with me. He looked thoughtful.

I continued complaining. 'I can't sleep on the bottom bunk either; I'm claustrophobic and the bunks don't look all that strong and I'm scared your great weight will come crashing down on me in the middle of the night and I'll be squashed to death.' I was almost enjoying this unusual-for-me bout of pessimism and determined to milk it for a while. Geoffrey continued staring at the bunks.

'What are we going to do?' I whined and he looked thoughtful for another moment or two before replying: 'I'll dismantle the bunks, put the upper mattress on the floor; you can sleep on the floor and I'll sleep on the lower bunk. There will be enough room if we take the chest of drawers out and put it on the landing and even more room if we remove the clothes rack and take that big stuffed Mickey Mouse out of here. If we put all of our clothes out on the landing and store our cases down in the garage, we'll be sweet.' He now had a determined gleam in his eye. Then he added cheerfully. 'You okay with all that?'

I got over my pessimism immediately and we set about rearranging the room. As well as sleeping on the floor, Geoffrey and

I were now required to share a bathroom with Ted. I had already warned Ted downstairs while he had his head in the washing machine, that I expected a clean and neat bathroom at all times and if I ever once found the toilet seat up, he would be missing a body part, probably the one he was most fond of.

I was later deeply ashamed when it turned out Ted was a man of immaculate bathroom manners. While all my old-lady accessories—indigestion tablets, make-up, shampoo, conditioner, body lotion, hair product, hair dryer, exfoliating gloves, body polish, dental floss, foundation, eye shadow, fungus ointment, mascara, hormone pills, hair brushes and gum massagers—cluttered up the bathroom, not even a toothbrush did Ted leave out. He left the bathroom spotless after using it for the quickest of times each day and never once did he leave the toilet seat up. I told him I wanted to marry him.

Later in the evening the weather turned cool and everyone huddled under the large gas heater on the upper terrace. Joanne arrived with her husband Peter to cook for us. Joanne is an English beauty; I'd call her an English rose except I think roses have to be pale, blonde things, whereas Joanne is dark with swinging chestnut hair and a bubbly expression on her lovely face. It's her lilting English accent that puts me in mind of an English rose. She and Peter have been living in France for six years where she runs a catering business.

She gave me a brief history of their life in France. 'We originally rented a house west of Montpellier, but it was not the France we had dreamed of, she said. 'It was difficult choosing a place as we had no actual job or reason to come here so we had the whole country to choose from. Fortunately, we found out about a truffle fair in Uzès, visited it and that was it.

'We love it here. I'm not saying that things are always easy and we still struggle with the language and to make ourselves understood, but you can get a lot from at least trying and smiling and giving lots of '*mercis*' and flirting.' (Had she been having lessons from Amanda?) 'We have an expression here: "you get more from licking than biting" and it seems to work particularly well. My French is slightly better than Peter's, but before we met I did have two French boyfriends which always makes you try harder.'

Joanne and Peter are probably not typical of the many English sea-changers who have taken up residence in France. They have tried to fit in with the local community, preferring to keep their friendship circles broad rather than staying in English cliques.

'Living here on a permanent basis is not actually better than living in the UK,' she said. 'But it certainly suits us better. The climate of course makes a difference, but there are lots of other things we appreciate. The sense of space compared to the overcrowded UK and the attitude here; it's much more relaxed and less competitive and not so commercial. The two-hour lunch break always calms everyone down, but it can be frustrating when you need to shop, everything is closed for lunch. But it's an excuse for a meal and another glass of wine and that makes up for any frustration over closed shops.'

Joanne had come to demonstrate the ease with which a host can bring an appealing meal to the table. She and Peter busied themselves in the kitchen while our guests enjoyed more wine on the terrace. Joanne had set the table in a tropical manner with flat green leaves running down the centre of the table. 'I always like to theme a dinner,' she explained when she came outside. 'Tonight I've done a mélange of food, a mixture of Thai, Italian, Chinese.' That Joanne could find ingredients for Thai or Chinese food in the French countryside was a triumph. I've spoken to Australian chefs in the past who said they had worked and cooked in France and Greece and had never found a red curry paste or tamarind water or been able to hunt down a kaffir lime leaf. But Joanne had discovered an Asian shop in the south of France and she was determined to introduce her French friends to food from outside their country.

'I've made Bloody Mary tomatoes,' she said and held up a plate of plump red tomatoes. 'I scooped out the middle and mixed the pulp with vodka and cayenne pepper and other Bloody Mary ingredients and put the mix back in. Next we have kebabs with black peppercorns served with raita. Then parmesan biscuits, which are really easy to do. You can prepare them weeks before, make up the mixture with parmesan cheese, butter and flour and roll it in a sausage and store it in the fridge. Then you can pull it out and slice it into rounds and bake them. They go well topped with chutney or pesto or goat cheese.'

It was pleasant watching Joanne. Her chestnut hair swung and bounced as she talked and her low-cut white top revealed a beautiful cleavage. I can't remember when I had been in front of so many great breasts ... which has nothing to do with cooking so let's hear what else Joanne had to say.

'These are prawn kebabs,' she continued. 'And these are sesame biscuits, very easy. I smother them with wasabi and rare roast beef. Then I have these filo pastries, they're very Moroccan.'

She looked lewdly at Amanda when she said this. She had obviously been privy to Amanda's tales of sexual athletics with the Moroccan lover. (Discretion is not a word familiar to Amanda when it comes to sharing tales of her sexual escapades.) Amanda just laughed and listened to Joanne's demonstration. 'Then we have spicy meatballs with rosemary skewers and finally Thai chicken balls.'

It was an exotic banquet in rural France, and after questions from everyone, Joanne finally sat to eat with us and continued chatting about her life in France. 'There does seem to be an old-fashioned sense of politeness here.' she said. 'For example, there is not a direct translation for *Monsieur* or *Madame* which is used here all the time, and there is definitely more acknowledgement of each other. Even when passing a child in the street you will be greeted with '*bonjour*'.

'There is an expression I'm sure you know: "The French cook to show off their skill, the Italians cook to show off their ingredients", meaning we think the French take their food, wine and cooking very seriously. People may not eat out as much as they do in Australia or the UK, say, but when they do it is often a five-course gourmet affair. Even dinner with our French friends is apéritifs, either pastis or spirits, followed by entrée, main course followed by salad, cheese and dessert and gallons of wine. Before we came here supper for us was just that—supper, one course, no dessert. We don't mind that now; an afternoon cooking with fresh ingredients, a bottle of wine and the inevitable argument about what to cook is what we love and why we're here.

'Ingredients here are very seasonal and preferably local. We have seen people throwing vegetables back on the supermarket counter when they realise that they are not French—especially if they're Spanish or even worse Dutch.' It was all an interesting insight into life in this area.

As we finished eating the Irish soap actor arrived again with red wine-stained lips and two bottles of wine under his arm. He came with several other people who I vaguely recalled meeting the night before. It all became very confused and then Ciara our kitchen hand threw a tantrum. I walked in on her and Amanda in torrid discussion in the kitchen.

'I don't know exactly what you want me to do, Amanda,' Ciara demanded tearfully. She had just returned from storming out of the kitchen to the garden where she had told someone to go fuck himself. (She said it in French, it sounded much prettier.)

Amanda was calm. 'You have to clear the table, help the chefs, wash up and leave the kitchen tidy,' she patiently explained to Ciara, which I think was pretty obvious when you hire someone to clear the table, help the chefs, wash up and leave the kitchen tidy.

'But part of my job should be to keep up the banter with the tour guests,' Ciara demanded in her lyrical accent.

'What?' asked Amanda, perplexed. 'I don't think I put "banter" on the job description.'

Ciara blew her nose. 'But it is important for me to have the banter with the guests,' she replied and then marched off to pour herself another glass of wine. When she was working and doing the duties she was paid to do, she was very good. She just did not see herself as a kitchenhand, more of a New York, A-list, Champagne-drinking, socialite hostess.

Added to the small problem of Ciara's above-her-station attitude was where to house her. She lived in Avignon, a 30-minute drive away with no car and no public transport to get her back and forth every day. She had to rely on us to pick her up and take her home which was completely unacceptable when we could barely get ourselves up and ready for the guests each day. Village friends of Amanda's had agreed to give Ciara a room in their apartment when they could and Hester had also agreed to house her at Ab Fab if there was a free room. But even that didn't completely solve the problem. Ciara had exam deadlines to attend to in Aix-en-Provence and there would be a number of occasions when she would have to be ferried back and forth to the city.

With all the other myriad arrangements Amanda kept making with unknown people on her mobile phone throughout each day, it was just another confusion that put my head in a spin. I can't recall the last time I felt so out of control and bewildered by all the happenings around me. And now, living in a tiny bunk room with a mattress on the floor, separated from my clothes, I couldn't find anything co-ordinated to wear. I looked a mess. It wasn't good. But the guests did not know that, would never know that. They were all so very happy and that alone was worth sleeping on the floor for and appearing dressed like a mad woman each morning.

After dinner Maurice strapped on the piano accordion and everyone filed into the warm kitchen of the big house for more music and dancing.

The night rollicked on. I did an ungainly version of the can can and danced with Ted holding his head between my breasts which is as far as it reached, for I am very tall and he is not. We sang *When the Saints Come Marching In* five times, Maurice did a little twirly dance on his own and the piano accordion nearly fell off, Françoise tried to clean up, Sharon went to her room and returned wearing the fur stole and beret purchased at the flea market and danced an energetic little shoulder-shimmying number. She looked so good we all had a turn at dancing in the hat and stole. Geoffrey thought about making another trip to the wine cave but realised it would be shut at this hour, so went in search of a stash of red wine he had hidden some place so secret he couldn't remember. Hester came in with some New Zealand visitors she had staying at Ab Fab and we all sang *When The Saints Come Marching In* again.

Around one in the morning one of the ladies began scratching her head and someone suggested the old fur hat and the stole might actually contain fleas, and then we all became convinced we had a head full of fleas and I suggested everyone go to their beds, which they did, and then I remembered I had to help Jessica and Leith make up a bed on the living room floor so I sent Geoffrey off to find a mattress while I heaved furniture aside and tried to put a heavy coffee table up on the couch, and then Amanda went off to find sheets and blankets, and a short while later I believe everyone in the big house and the little house, as well as all the drop-ins still drinking out on the terrace and down in the walled garden, simultaneously fell into comas wherever they lay or stood.

5
Revenge of the Cretins

I don't think it will come as a surprise to you to learn that Amanda has problems with some of her neighbours. Although she is very popular in the village and the surrounding area, anyone living close to her is not particularly fond of her. It's all the partying of course, and the annoyance of her many visitors' cars choking the tiny square outside Maison de Maîtresse. The little square is actually a thoroughfare but many of her holiday tenants do not realise this and park their cars right out side Amanda's door, blocking the way through to narrow alleyways which are actually roads. Amanda has made every effort to educate her tenants and visitors about parked cars but the problem persists.

There have been neighbourhood arguments, especially with one man who she calls 'the cretin'. I believe there have been occasions when Amanda has charged out of her house wearing nothing but the green sarong to take up argument with the cretin over various matters ranging from blocked access ways to unacceptable noise levels. Threats have been made—of what nature I cannot be sure, perhaps by Amanda to charge out of the house completely naked if the cretin would not back down—and the *gendarme* has been called out on a number of occasions.

Another neighbour, Cretin Number Two, has also fallen foul of Amanda although he has not, to Amanda's knowledge, been responsible for calling out the *gendarme*. There are much more cunning and insidious ways to pay Amanda back for loud music and car doors slamming in the wee hours of the morning. Blocking the driveway into Amanda's garage with his own car is one way. But as Amanda can never use her garage because of the mountain of party accessories stored in it, the driveway is of no use to her anyway. I can only guess at what manner of *contretemps* occurred between Amanda and Cretin Number Two to cause such dislike but once, during a particularly feisty encounter in the village, Cretin Number Two threatened a jabbing action with his cigarette towards Amanda's bosom. Amanda never said whether the cigarette was alight or not but this gesture sealed the lid on a feud that would become a bitter enmity. You can argue with Amanda about party noise, berate her angrily over badly parked cars and call the *gendarme* out to quieten her, but you *never* mess with her bosom. She grabbed his wrist in a powerful grip and almost wrestled him to the ground. Now they have agreed to hate each other silently.

So, when our group emerged into the little village square this morning, ready for a day of lengthy excursion, to find one of the tyres on the mini-van completely flat with a large nail embedded in it, Amanda's first thought was: 'Revenge of the Cretins'. We had been particularly noisy, even by Amanda's standards, over the past few nights. 'It must have been done by one of them,' she pronounced, looking angrily at the flat tyre. 'I wouldn't put it past them.'

Of course such accusations could only be made under the breath, not in front of the group and certainly not to the cretins' faces. The last thing we wanted was for our group to be brought into a long-running, nasty neighbourhood argument. Geoffrey was of the opinion we had run over the nail on the road the day before. Amanda was not convinced. However, there was nothing she could do about it; no-one had witnessed a cretin creeping about the village armed with a nail gun the night before.

The group congregated around the flat tyre; aghast at the size of the nail and the total flatness of the tyre. Françoise and Maurice joined us and offered various opinions in rapid French which only Amanda understood. Hester came from next door and joined the inspection. Luce had plenty to say on the subject of flat tyres. A great deal of examination and summation took place until we all agreed we would never know how the nail got in the tyre and it didn't really matter anyway, it had to be fixed. Another of Geoffrey's many skills (aside from chauffering, hosting, and wine-buying) is that he can fix anything. He set to work while Amanda made several telephone calls and the group went back inside to gossip and wait.

Today we were to visit two towns, Roussillon and Gordes. Roussillon, only an hour away from St. Maximin sits on the southern edge of the Plateau de Vaucluse and is a highlight for any visitor to France. Its red ochre hills and disused quarry are set in deep green valleys and its medieval village sits on top of a green pine forest. Inside the village ochre-coloured buildings and narrow medieval streets offer interest at every turn. There were quality shops, excellent cafés and restaurants, a charming square, a handsome clock tower and an eleventh-century church to be inspected and enjoyed. After we had explored the park of red ochre hills we would have lunch in the village and then spend the afternoon in nearby Gordes, another ancient town of great history and Provençal charm.

Amanda had given us a briefing the night before. Her local knowledge was comprehensive and her recitation of historic facts impressive. She obviously felt passionate about this region and had taken many visitors to these towns before. She told us to wear sturdy footwear, as sandals would not be adequate for walking and keeping the red ochre dust from staining our feet. I had staggered up off the floor from the mattress this morning, aching, and foggy with lack of sleep, and could find nothing appropriate to wear in the jumble of clothes on the landing so I appeared wearing an outfit you might expect a little girl to wear after she had raided her mother's cupboards to play dress-up. I had on a pair of light stretchy brown three- quarter length pants, the kind that look good for a beach walk with a pair of thongs, not with a great big pair of black running shoes the size of small boats. On top I wore a light white T-shirt, and had taken, at the last minute, a red paisley fitted jacket. Everyone laughed at my outfit and commented on the large size of my feet. I tried to make lame excuses about not being able to find anything now that I had to sleep in a room and keep my clothes out on the landing, but I didn't want to make much of it for Gail and Joan's sake. No-one but Ted had been up to the top of the stairs in the big house and seen the tightness of the room Geoffrey and I were using. I wanted it to remain that way.

After Geoffrey had repaired the tyre and Amanda had made several dozen telephone calls involving arrangements for the day so complex they took my breath away, we set off in an untidy convoy: she and I in her silver car with Ciara lying across the narrow back seat; Geoffrey with the guests in the van; Maurice and Françoise with Jessica and Leith and their camera equipment in Maurice's car. It should have been easy had we all actually been going directly to Roussillon, but we weren't. Amanda and I had to drop Ciara off at the train station in Avignon and pick up Amanda's son, Piers, who was arriving from Sardinia where he had been working as a DJ. He was to spend the day and evening with Amanda. Maurice and Françoise, had to go to another station in Avignon to pick up Rosemary, their chef friend arriving from Spain. So many arrangements!

On the drive to Avignon Amanda's phone rang a half a dozen times and in between talking to lovers, she made yet more arrangements of a bewildering nature and invited several more people to join us for dinner that night. I tuned out. Her multifarious plans always worked out and trying to keep up with them and the constant changes she made to them only caused me stress and anxiety.

We dropped off Ciara who made no mention of or offered an apology for her tantrum the night before, and picked up Piers. Piers was a devilishly handsome young man with the same vibrant personality as his mother. With him now lying across the back seat and talking rapidly to his mother in between making calls on his own phone, we drove for an hour through plain countryside straight to Roussillon where, surprise, surprise, we actually met up with Geoffrey and the group immediately and without stress. We parked in the car park on top of the hill just outside the village near the entrance to the red ochre quarries.

'Where is the film crew?' Amanda demanded the minute we stepped out of the car and greeted the group. 'They were supposed to be here before us.'

No-one had an answer for her.

She then telephoned Maurice who informed her that Jessica, Leith, he and Françoise were still waiting at the station in Avignon for Rosemary's arrival and we should start the walk in the red ochre park without them. This was upsetting as our plan had been to get some spectacular footage in the park with the group against the backdrop of the extraordinary red hills. Amanda was discovering there were many obstacles and difficulties in filming a lifestyle documentary—obstacles I had foreseen, although not on this level.

While Piers introduced himself to the group, Amanda made several more phone calls and Geoffrey went off to buy tickets to get us all in the park.

Although the sky was a piercing blue, the weather had turned bitterly cold and an icy wind sliced through everyone's clothes, forcing them to fold their arms around their bodies and stamp their feet to try to keep warm. We were all inadequately dressed. I had told the group via email before we arrived in France to pack lightly. 'It's casual, no need to dress up,' I repeatedly encouraged them. 'The weather in Provence in summer stays the same every day. They have 300 days of sunshine every year, no need for any heavy clothes.' And so, on this icy cold day with the sharpest wind I had ever encountered—and I come from Melbourne and have visited San Francisco—everyone was dressed in light sweaters and pants, flowing skirts and cotton T-shirts.

'Let's start walking through the park, that will warm us,' I said with false cheer as Joan rummaged in her bag for a scarf to tie around her bare arms and Ted, the only smart one amongst us, pulled a windproof anorak out of his backpack. We filed into the park and it was every bit as spectacular as Amanda had said it would be. All of us, being Australians, could relate to the red ochre immediately, but here it rose in magnificent hills and mounds of twisted shapes. We walked along a boardwalk surrounded on each side by rolling red shapes from which sprouted vivid green growth. The deep-red colour was all the more breathtaking as we looked out over the park to the green valley undulating before us. We climbed the red hills, shivered, hugged our arms around our bodies, politely pretended to each other that it wasn't really that cold, and posed for group photos against many of the dramatic red backdrops.

'Don't say sex or cheese when you pose for photos,' Rosa advised. 'Say gorgonzola. It makes your mouth shape lovely.' So we all shouted 'gorgonzola' ten times, one for each of our cameras at each highlight, and generally annoyed all the other tourists in the park.

Joan was the first to get up the steepest hill, and quickest to discover a new path that led to more red hill formations. Ted, with his awkward leg never complained as he was made to climb difficult places I'm sure he would rather not have. Eve, the fittest in the group, looked like a triathlete as she rushed about, and despite the biting cold, we spent a thrilling hour amongst the red hills.

Finally, our other little group arrived with Rosemary. When Jessica and Leith saw the depth of the red and the stunning hills, they quickly set up the cameras and began filming. Amanda continued to make more phone calls. After a short while we decided it was time to eat and drink again and so set off out of the park for the village.

Today was to be one of only three occasions during the entire tour where the group would have to find lunch on their own. Amanda told them there were many cafés in the village and we arranged to meet back at the car park at 2pm.

Everybody broke up and went their separate ways. By now Joan and Shirley had bonded and were already a duo. Margaret and Sharon had formed a friendship and were fast becoming inseparable. Gail was happy to join in with anyone.

While Jessica and Leith continued filming in the park, Amanda and her son walked to the village and Geoffrey and I hurried off separately, hoping it might be a little warmer inside the tight and narrow streets of the village.

Roussillon is a typical Provençal village of charming art galleries representing local artists and small boutiques selling good souvenirs and bags of aromatic lavender, a dream to anyone who has ever picked up a paintbrush or shown an interest in photography. We poked around the shops for a short while and made our way to the village centre where we found the entire group had joined up to lunch together in the same little bistro. There were dozens of similar bistros to choose from, yet here they all were, sitting at the same place with two tables pushed together.

'I thought you would enjoy some free time away from each other,' I said, astonished, but in a delighted way.

'No, we like each other,' they replied and I was struck by how lucky I was to have landed a group, on my very first tour, who got on so well with each other. I found it immensely heartening to see that when they did have the opportunity to put some space between themselves, they chose not to.

They were all eating salads, quiches, onion tarts and fat sausages and we joined them, ordering Mediterranean tarts with rustic salad. We shivered our way through lunch.

Rosa had already found a designer shop and bought herself an expensive outfit, a cream linen top and skirt with a cheerful modern print. Everybody but Ted and Geoffrey admired her outfit as she took it from the bag to show us in the bistro and I suspect we all shared the same thought: did she buy it especially to wear tonight for the reunion with her separated husband?

After lunch we had only 15 minutes to wander and film before it was time to assemble at the car park. By now several members of the group had bought warm sweaters and scarves and were feeling much better. They continued to tease me about my weird outfit.

I was paranoid about being on time to meet them by the van. The exposed car park on top of the hill had to be the coldest, windiest place in the world today. Geoffrey and I arrived five minutes early, hugged each other tightly against the wind and did a kind of stomping dance in a useless attempt to keep warm. So anxious were we waiting for the group to arrive we didn't even think of getting inside the van for warmth. We have a way to go yet before we become savvy tour guides.

Once everybody was rounded up and I had managed to find those stragglers who had discovered a tempting art gallery just near the car park, we set off in an ordered convoy. I found myself in Maurice's car in the back seat with Sharon and now Rosemary, the Spanish chef. I cannot recall why we all changed cars, it was all part of the confusion. Rosemary sat between Sharon and me and without a word of English, had no choice but to smile pleasantly for the short half-hour drive to Gordes.

Built on the foothills of the Monts of Vaucluse, facing the Luberon valley, Gordes is one of France's most well-known hilltop villages and one of its prettiest. Its grey stone houses and buildings appear to have taken root in the sharp mountain-face, and cling dramatically halfway down the mountain. This is the village that has inspired many famous artists in Provence, and anyone who has ever visited Gordes will understand why. It is seen at its most dramatic from the approaching road where many a postcard photo has been taken. To walk the labyrinth of medieval streets in these Provençal villages is to feel history all around you—the architecture is breathtaking, the handsome buildings fascinating.

Not today for us, however. Today in Gordes the rain fell heavily and the cutting wind had become fierce. Even to get out of the car required an act of small bravery. Once our convoy had driven as high into the centre of the village as cars could go, it was tempting just to sit inside the car and pretend we had visited Gordes.

Outside, a few tourists who had braved the weather were being blown along the streets, their umbrellas turning inside out. I felt personally responsible for the weather.

It is that annoying trait in my character that makes me want everything to be perfect when I entertain guests. You will have experienced this feeling if you've ever hosted an outdoor event and rain or wind has spoiled your plans. Now, with this foul weather I could have wept, but that would have been senseless and way too girly. Instead, I braced myself, got out of the car and encouraged the others in the van to do the same.

'We'll stay just 15 minutes,' I mouthed as they peered miserably at me through the van windows. 'You must get out and have a look. It's the most beautiful hilltop town in France.'

They didn't believe me, but soon, everyone was out, bent over against the strong wind and sleeting rain, and rushing for the nearest shop. Thank God for shops; they must have saved many a tour guide from the burden of responsibility on rainy days.

We all crowded into a snug shop and within minutes everyone was engrossed in the subject of honey and liquorice, oblivious to the water dripping off their noses. Honey, calendars, postcards, lavender soaps and liquorice were all purchased and strangely, yet again, everyone in the group seemed feverishly happy. I loved them for their enthusiasm and lack of complaint.

Geoffrey came in bouncing and dripping five minutes later telling us he had been down a tight cobbled laneway that opened out to a narrow stone road clinging to the cliff where the view of the Lubéron below was so vast and stunning, it was worth a few wet minutes.

'You must all go down and check out the view,' he said. 'It would be such a shame to miss it.'

Some people lowered their heads to the honey and postcards and pretended they didn't hear him, but Joan rushed out of the shop, followed closely by Gail and Eve the triathlete. I joined them, staying close to the side of the old walls in the alleyway, my head bent against the rain. In a few saturating minutes we had made it down the road and stood with other hardy tourists for as long as we could bear, admiring the sprawling green valley stretching to the horizon. Even in the miserable rain it looked like an exquisite oil painting.

Reluctantly we left Gordes; the shocking weather had prevented us from fully appreciating its charms and there wasn't much else to do unless we wanted to sit inside the cars looking at the ancient village through the windows.

We drove out of town, pulled over to the side of the road to look back and admire the view and everyone decided they had to have a group shot with the striking Gordes backdrop. The rain eased for a moment and so after posing for each of our cameras, and after ten more loud exclamations of 'gorgonzola' we all tramped wetly back to the cars to prepare for home. Maurice, however, suggested that we should visit Fontaine-de-Vaucluse, another medieval village not far away in the valley of the Plateau de Vaucluse.

'We are so close,' he said as he got out his map and spread it over the dashboard. 'It would be a shame not to visit now.' We put it to the vote, as some of the group were reluctant to continue in such miserable weather. But a visit to Fontaine-de-Vaucluse won.

All I wanted to do was to go back to Maison de Maîtresse, get out of my ridiculous damp outfit and get into a glass or three of rosé. But off we went, and within 15 minutes we stopped in convoy in the centre of town looking for a car park where there was none. Maurice got out and walked over to a nearby *gendarme* whereupon one of those wonderfully European discussions began. We watched from the car as much arm-waving and hand-gesticulating took place for at least five lively minutes until Maurice came back and announced we could all leave our cars and the van right there in the middle of the main square where they stood.

'What did you tell him?' I asked, impressed and pleased. It meant we would have to walk only a few minutes to the pedestrianised area which was obviously the hub of all activity.

'I told him you were a VIP group from Australia here to film for an important television documentary,' he said without blushing, and we all climbed out and walked happily into the tourist strip running parallel to a fast-flowing, creamy-blue river.

All the typical tourist shops lined the strip—ice-cream outlets, souvenir stands and expensive restaurants—but it was very attractive. The rain was light now, but the skies were overcast and I silently pleaded for the sun to come out so we could enjoy this pretty spot.

Fontaine-de-Vaucluse lies at the base of high rocky cliffs, squeezed into the sharp end of a narrow valley. Its name comes from the mysterious spring feeding the river Sorgue which dominates the town. This spring forms the crystal-clear river which turns a startling emerald and then a vivid blue as it flows.

The spring comes up from underground and no-one knows how deep it runs. In the 1950s the French underwater explorer Jacques Cousteau came to the area with a submersible to explore the depths. Not even he found the bottom. We could have walked to the spring but Amanda strongly advised against it. 'It would take half an hour and the weather is not good for such a walk,' she warned and everyone was grateful.

Instead, we walked the strip by the river, stopping briefly at the shops and peering into the restaurants built out over the water. It was very picturesque and we wandered to the end into a covered arcade, the Vallis Clausa, where we found the most beautiful sweet shop in the world. Giant meringues the size of small hills were piled in snowy-white mountains at the front of the shop and led the sweet tooths amongst us inside to a chocoholic's paradise. Great slabs of dark, milk and white chocolate and bars of caramel toffee were beautifully displayed. I bought a dozen meringues for our dessert tonight even though the proprietor warned me a couple would be enough to feed ten people.

At the end of the Vallis Clausa, we came to the fourteenth-century paper mill that is still a working mill today but is known more now as a tourist attraction. We explored the museum and examined beautiful paper made in the traditional way of centuries ago. We all stopped to look at the giant paddle wheel that once harnessed the river's power to make the paper. We spent as much time as we decently could admiring the paper but most of the guests were anxious to get home now. It had been a long day and we had another gourmet dinner to look forward to. And we had the arrival of Gino to contemplate.

6

The Mistral and the Soufflé

After we arrived back from Fontaine-de-Vaucluse, Maurice told us the formidable Mistral was responsible for the unusual cold snap. The Mistral is a cold, fierce wind that blows through the Rhône valley to the Med, usually in the winter and spring. He said he had never known it this cold in June. I took it personally. The Mistral had come to Provence in summer to deliberately sabotage my inaugural tour. Maurice tried to comfort me with his Mistral knowledge.

'They say a Mistral lasts for three, six or nine days,' he said rather too cheerfully. 'If it goes the day after tomorrow we are safe, if not, well ... ' His gorgeous accent somehow made this terrible news sound romantic.

Anyone who knows about Provence knows about the Mistral. We all read about it in Peter Mayle's glorious book *A Year in Provence*, where he experienced its full force during the second month after his arrival. He told us how the locals said a Mistral could blow the ears off a donkey and while that was fun and informative to read inside my cosy home in Australia, it was anything but fun now— and it had happened to Peter Mayle in February, not June. I silently prayed for a three-day Mistral and left Maurice, rushing to Amanda's apartment seeking to borrow warm clothing for all of us. She was busy talking to Piers, but took down all the lurid boas, vivid shawls, multi-coloured scarves and the crimson wrap from her bedroom screen and handed the colourful bundle to me. When I carried it upstairs to the terrace where everyone had gathered under the gas heater, they pounced gratefully on the dazzling garments and immediately wrapped themselves in garish warmth. We looked like escapees from a South American brothel. Someone had a pink boa around her neck, another had a crimson wrap over her shoulders, someone else had a bright purple scarf slung across her back. Ted looked particularly ridiculous in the white pompom wrap. On top of his ubiquitous shorts, the pompoms dangled obscenely down to his knees; the look was so preposterous it was actually quite wonderful. Geoffrey, looking most fetching in a mauve boa, poured wine to help warm everyone on the inside.

It was another night of sublime food and copious wine. Romantic dramas might occur, arguments in the kitchen were inevitable and if a man had to wear a white wrap with dangling pompoms, then so be it. But as long as there was good food and access to unlimited wine, we could cope with anything. Françoise was preparing frogs' legs, quenelles and a duck liver soufflé for our dinner. We let her get on with it and huddled together with our wine glasses.

Within ten minutes we knew we had to eat inside; it would be far too cold to sit out, even with the spreading warmth from the big overhead gas heater. The kitchen in the big house was full of cooks; the living room had been taken over as a bedroom by Jessica and Leith so we all piled in to the cosy eating area of the kitchen in La Petite Maison, the small house. The table could sit ten at a squeeze and it was so comfy and intimate we could rid ourselves of our flashy costumes and crowd around the table in a close and happy group. Rosa was wearing another glamorous outfit and while we waited for the arrival of both Gino and our dinner, we drank far too much wine. It became raucous once again. Amanda entertained everyone with colourful stories about her Moroccan lover who she calls *Chocolat* because of his smooth chocolate voice. She had so wanted *Chocolat* to come to France to join in the tour—to show him off to the ladies in other words—but she'd encountered obstacles with the French public servants. She had been to every authority in the country to plead his case; she had presented an impressive amount of documents to prove he would not be a burden on anyone in France for the two weeks of his stay. After being told to go away and wait, she had been patient for weeks, waiting on replies that never came. She made countless telephone calls to bureaucrats, all without success. Her last effort to get *Chocolat* to France had entailed her having to post her passport to him so he could present it to the authorities in Morocco. She now told the group the story. Ted, who had no interest in Amanda's sex life wandered off to offer cooking assistance to Françoise, Maurice, Rosemary and Luce, and film assistance to Jessica and Leith. I will say no more on that subject.

'I did not want *Chocolat* to see my passport,' Amanda told the ladies as she showed them a photo of the handsome 40-year-old who looked even more dashing than the truck tryst man. 'If he saw my passport he would find out my age,' she continued, at which the women clutched each other laughing. 'I put the passport inside a sealed envelope inside another envelope before I posted it to him and told him the seal could not be broken as the authorities would suspect foul play and that he had to take it intact and hand it over to them, and only them, without looking at it.' There was much laughing and spluttering at the table over this. We all looked at Amanda with deep admiration. She had a handsome and exotic lover more than 20 years her junior and he obviously had the discretion and good manners not to ask about her age. I think every woman at the table that night, apart from me, had the thought of taking on a much younger man in a quest to bring out her true inner vamp. (Actually, I can't lie; I did too. Don't mention it to Geoffrey though.)

'I am a *salope*, a *dragueuse*,' Amanda said. 'They are French words for flirt and slut. They sound so much better in French, don't they? You can call me *une dragueuse*, I don't mind.'

We continued talking and laughing about sex, ageing women and younger men, until Françoise and her entourage made a grand entrance with a magnificently risen soufflé. Rowdy cries of 'bravo' greeted the soufflé as Françoise placed it in the centre of the table and dug a spoon deep into its middle. Our cheers of appreciation were quickly followed by her anguished cries of alarm as she realised the soufflé was not thoroughly baked. She went to remove it from the table.

'We don't care,' we shouted, full of boozy bonhomie. 'It will be perfect,' but she would not permit us to eat an inferior soufflé, and she whisked it off the table and headed back into the other kitchen. Her entourage followed.

'It's the oven,' Maurice called over his shoulder as he followed the soufflé procession out the door. 'Françoise is not used to this oven. At home her soufflés always rise perfectly and behave well.'

As the evening continued in its rowdy way most of us forgot about Gino, and when the frogs' legs were carried in with due ceremony all thoughts of anything but culinary bravery disappeared. Everyone was hesitant to start eating; the crumbed frogs' legs looked so innocent and small. Sharon refused to even try one. 'I had a cute green frog at home once,' she said and watched while the others all gamely picked up a tiny leg and cautiously put it to their lips.

I had enough wine in me to have a go at anything, even a plate of chargrilled witchetty grubs would have been appealing right then, and before I realised it, I'd eaten four of the tiny legs. They tasted almost the same as chicken, quite delicate but more chewy. Maurice, obviously a devotee of the frog leg (or *cuisses de grenouilles* as they are known in France meaning frogs' thighs) smacked his fingers to his lips in an appreciative gesture as he told us to enjoy them. There was so little meat on each leg it required the consumption of twenty or more to feel any satisfaction. I tucked in heartily while the others all nibbled politely.

Amanda had mysteriously disappeared, and I assumed it was because French though she appeared with her fluency of the language and knowledge of the area, she did not favour eating the tiny legs off little green frogs.

A short while later the soufflé made another grand entrance and once again there were boozy shouts of *'bravo'* as it was placed carefully in the middle of the table. Everyone in the group showed respectful silence as Françoise dug the spoon into its centre for the second time that evening, and then let out another bawdy *'bravo'* as she declared the centre perfectly cooked.

The soufflé was a stunning success considering this, the most fragile of all dishes, had travelled backwards and forwards over the terrace three times from the kitchen of the big house to the kitchen of the small house in the midst of a Mistral. She spooned out big dollops of the delicate custardy mixture while Maurice dished up the fat quenelles coated in a rich tomato sauce. We all gave the delicious food our respect and proper attention for the next half hour.

Amanda came back and whispered to me that a drama was unfolding. Gino, who had been travelling from Australia for almost 30 hours had arrived in Avignon, picked up his hire car and telephoned Amanda who had given him clear instructions on how to drive to St. Maximin. However, what she had not told him was there were two villages called St. Maximin in France … .the other one a three-hour drive in the wrong direction. This dashing romeo, who had travelled across the world seeking reconciliation and romance, was now three hours away across the region. He had gone to St. Maximin-la-Sainte-Baume.

Catastrophe!

Rosa was looking calm and lovely, with no idea of the calamity occurring. Amanda was genuinely concerned for Gino but the half litre of wine she'd consumed was doing an excellent job of containing her guilt. She murmured something about it being his fault for not listening properly. St. Maximin-la-Sainte-Baume, as everybody knew, was the place where Mary Magdalene was rehabilitated in the thirteenth century and remade as the sinning figure of perfect penitence. But it wasn't her St. Maximin. She poured another glass of wine to wash away any last hint of her distress and declared her intention to party on. Everyone followed suit, and three hours passed quickly as they do when you are drinking French wine and enjoying good company, and before we realised it poor Gino was downstairs ringing the bell to Amanda's front door while party pandemonium reigned upstairs. Tiny frog bones were scattered all over the table, the dregs of liver soufflé lay on uncleared plates, tomato sauce was splashed over the tablecloth, half-filled and empty wine glasses sat accusingly on every bit of bench space, and many lips and teeth were stained with red wine. The piano accordion had long ago been cranked up; no-one was thinking about retiring for the night. Ciara our kitchen hand was decidedly absent. Piers had popped his head in once or twice and then fled in alarm.

Amanda slipped quietly away to let Gino in but returned alone. She whispered to me. 'Gino has arrived but he looked so travel weary and scruffy I sent him away again.' Her voice was very low; she did not want the other guests to know of his drive all over France.

I was incredulous. 'You sent him away? After he'd flown all this way from Australia and driven halfway around France?'

'I had to,' she replied quietly. 'I did not want a romantic reunion with him looking so bedraggled. I told him Rosa would not want to see him looking scruffy.'

Looking at Rosa's immaculate appearance I could understand that, but still, sending him away after all he'd been through ... ?

'What's he look like?' I asked, suddenly very curious.

'Nice looking but not tall,' Amanda said and then we forgot about him as another chorus of *When the Saints Go Marching In* had struck up again.

Half an hour later Amanda disappeared yet again and came back agitated.

'Gino has just returned looking as scruffy and bedraggled as he did before so I sent him away,' she said.

I didn't know what to say. It was now well into the wee hours of the morning and the romantic reunion we had all anticipated had been forgotten by everyone but poor Gino.

'He couldn't find his hotel down the road,' Amanda continued.

'So he came back here and I told him to go again.' She looked around the room for more wine, dismissing any more thoughts of Gino.

We did not hear from him again. It turned out he had finally found his hotel, woken up the proprietors, got to his room, sat down on the bed before contemplating a shower, and fallen back on the pillows where he lay in his travel-stained clothes for a long and very deep sleep.

We did not find this out until the next morning at breakfast and Rosa never inquired as to his whereabouts.

After the long day of touring yesterday and another big night of food, wine and song, everyone was pleased not to have to tour again today, although not so pleased with the cold wind. Lounging by the pool after another French lesson with Maurice over breakfast had been our plan but now most of the guests were trying to find a sheltered spot in the garden out of the Mistral.

A few guests stayed on in the kitchen with Maurice where he was happy to give extended French lessons.

He talked of vowels, of past and present tense, of singular and plural sentences, of grammatical correctness. 'Am I going too fast? *Comment allez-vous?* Are you writing this down? It is important.' Sharon and Rosa were listening to him avidly when Amanda entered the kitchen wearing a short leopard-print slip, the remnants of last night's makeup all over her face and her blonde streaked hair in wild disarray. Her unsecured breasts were on the verge of falling out of the low-cut slip but seeing as everyone was so used to them by now, no-one took the slightest notice. On her arm was Gino, a delicate and diminutive man with glasses, thick wavy hair and the very definite air of a rabbit caught in the headlights. Everyone went silent and stared at him.

'Well, aren't you going to hug your wife,' Amanda finally said and pushed him towards Rosa who got up to embrace him. Everyone wept, except Rosa. Amanda was uncharacteristically overcome. She stood in the middle of the room, hung-over and semi-naked, sobbing for a couple she barely knew.

The others, outside hunting for a wind-free spot, were upset at having missed the reunion, but Rosa took Gino out and introduced him to everyone. He shyly shook hands and looked longingly at Rosa.

The whole Rosa and Gino episode had turned out to be quite the anticlimax. Everyone had been anticipating it yesterday with great excitement but now he was actually here, romance had been all but forgotten and other matters, such as recovery from the night before and shelter from the Mistral, took on more importance. Although everyone greeted Gino warmly, they quickly turned their attention to matters of their own comfort.

Chef Dean arrived from the boat on the Canal du Midi. He was going to show us how to make a *pissaladière*, a traditional French onion and anchovy tart. Amanda and I took him to the kitchen where Françoise and Rosemary greeted him with suspicion.

I love this salty, flavoursome tart and have often made it for dinner guests to eat with pre-dinner drinks. It can be complicated if you are of a nature to make everything from scratch, but if you take shortcuts it is easy. Dean was not taking shortcuts. After the guests had piled into the kitchen in the big house and were seated around the table, he began his demonstration with puff pastry making.

Watching Dean cut up cubes of unsalted butter and chop them into the flour brought a flood of schoolgirl memories back to me. Making puff pastry was a rite of passage for women of my generation and I enjoyed Dean's demonstration immensely. I don't think the same could be said for Françoise who was showing signs of impatience and talking to Amanda in French while Dean rolled pastry and prepared onions.

She was, Amanda told me later, concerned that Dean's demonstration was going on too long and the guests would be hungry. Seeing as they had finished breakfast very late it was obviously not a problem and besides, they were all sitting at the table with a glass of wine before them. But this was not good enough for Françoise who loved nothing more than to see people eating. She bustled to the fridge to find a tapenade Amanda made the day before and put it on the table.

It was three in the afternoon by the time Dean chopped and sautéed the onions to a caramelised texture, spread them on the pastry squares, topped them decoratively with anchovies and black olives and put the tarts in the oven.

Amanda left to take Piers back to the Avignon train station. Hester turned up with a bottle of wine. She could tell immediately that no-one was expecting her.

'Did Amanda not tell anyone she invited me?' Hester asked and I couldn't help but laugh. It was so typical of all the arrangements that took place every day. Rarely did anyone in the house know the full extent of Amanda's plans.

'I never know what's going on here,' I told Hester. 'But it's all part of the fun and everything works out in the end. Let's open your bottle of wine.'

We poured a drink and Hester told me how she had been drawn into our tour project in a roundabout way by Amanda as we needed Hester's accommodation at Ab Fab for the visiting chefs.

'I was told to prepare one of the apartments for a male chef,' Hester said. 'I presumed it was Dean so I put a masculine bedspread on the bed, took out anything girly, made sure everything was neat and tidy and welcoming for him and then Rosemary turned up at my door with her suitcase.'

I laughed until I ached. I did not dare ask where Dean would sleep that night. He was busy making another batch of puff pastry and chopping more onions for another lot of tarts in case anyone else unexpectedly turned up.

By the time we sat down to lunch it was very late but the *pissaladière* was a hit. Served with an endive and radish salad dressed with a simple vinaigrette, it was another victory. The saltiness of the olives and anchovies contrasted with the buttery pastry and filled the mouth with flavour. The clean, fresh, perfectly dressed salad was just the right balance. The French do not mess about with salad dressings. They would be horrified at the thought of fish sauce, chilli or coriander in a salad dressing. They use only olive oil, red or white wine vinegar, Dijon mustard, garlic and seasoning. Amanda makes one of the best dressings I've ever tasted. She puts one other ingredient into the basic vinaigrette recipe and will not tell me what it is. She makes her dressing in the bowl she will serve the salad in and after she has piled the salad ingredients on top, it goes to table. She tosses the salad only seconds before serving it. Her salads are the best I've ever experienced.

And while I am talking about her cooking prowess, let me tell you about her tapenade. She makes it with green olives, ground almonds, olive oil, garlic, capers and anchovies. Once she has assembled all the ingredients, it takes her only minutes to whip up a big batch of tapenade for any extra people who turn up throughout the day or evening. Seeing as this is the case every day of her life, she makes a lot of tapenade. She serves it with chunks of baguette and it goes a long way.

These past few days my taste buds have been opened as I would never have believed possible. Each meal has been memorable. The produce has been fresh, flavoursome and allowed to shine without fuss or trickery from our chefs. Our guests feel the same way … and we have yet to take them to the Uzès markets to experience the bounty of food and produce there.

7
The Uzès Markets

At the risk of sounding like a complaining old so and so, let me have a little moan. As I have already indicated, here at Maison de Maîtresse small routine acts have become complicated feats for me. Finding clothes that might match even reasonably well in the jumble on the landing is so difficult I have resigned myself to wearing the same thing every day. This is nothing compared to the difficult act of getting in and out of both houses. Before you get annoyed with me—I mean, who'd blame you, a grown woman calling herself a tour guide who can't dress herself nicely or get out of a couple of houses—let me explain.

Amanda is paranoid about security; she has insisted on locking everything down tighter than a high-security prison ever since her house was burgled one night while she and 20 mates were partying hard upstairs. A lot of money, jewellery and a computer were stolen. So now every door and window in both houses is bolted and locked with a fearsome set of keys even a jailer would find complicated. The front door lock in the big house requires the key to be jiggled in a series of mysterious ways before the door will actually unlock. And the key, which is supposed to live in the door for easy locating for the duration of this tour, is rarely in the door. One or two of the group might have taken it when they've gone for a walk in the village, something I have yet had the time for, or someone may have used it and not put it back in the lock.

In the small house, the front door is much easier to open but to get to it, I have to go through Amanda's bedroom and kitchen and up the stairs lined with the shelves of pantry goods. The key for this door is supposed to live in a glass dish on a table by the door, but with so many people coming and going, of course, it is never there. Amanda has brought out two spare sets of keys already, both of which have disappeared. Hunting down keys has become her personal nightmare.

Almost every time I have shimmied sideways up the stairs past the stacked shelves on the narrow staircase, brushing up against sticky jars of pantry goods, I have arrived at the front door with my boobs smeared with oil and vinegar, to find no key available to get out. I then have to slither back down past the pantry goods again, into Amanda's kitchen, down the step through to her bedroom to often find myself actually trapped in there because Amanda has gone out into the garden and locked the formidable iron bars over her garden door exit. Getting around both houses without your own set of keys on your person at all times requires the skills of a jailor and the spirit of a pioneer. However, the guests don't seem to have any trouble at all. They pop in and go out with ease and they seem to know the geography of the property as if they have lived there for years. I, on the other hand, fumble my way around the property contemplating scaling walls and battering down doors to get in or out. There have been times these past few days, in moments of silly self-pity, when I think I must be quite mad for embarking on this new career as tour leader at my late stage in life. If I cannot look after myself properly, how can I be expected to look after others?

But those self-pitying moments last only as long as it takes for someone to pour another glass of pink wine or for Maurice to pick up the piano accordion once more. I am really having the most wonderful time I have ever experienced in all my travels. Every day has been a joy. Hold that thought for a moment because I haven't finished complaining.

I have encountered a quirky problem with the hair dryer. There is no power point in the bathroom I share with Geoffrey and Ted, and there is so much stuff and not enough space in the bunk room I couldn't even try to look for one there. However, Shirley has kindly let me use her bathroom for the purpose of styling my hair each morning. This brings forth another set of complications. Her bathroom has been newly built on to the big house and juts out and hangs in the air like a little sunken balcony. You must step down a steep step off the landing to get into it. Although the bathroom is quite narrow, it is light and airy with a small window looking out over the pool and garden. The power point is on the floor at the bottom of the steep step just inside the door. To plug in the hair dryer, I have to lie flat on the floor on the landing with my head hanging down over the bathroom step, groping blindly around the floor trying to locate the socket. It is not my most attractive position and one I would rather not have Ted find me in most mornings as he makes his difficult way down the steps. And then there is the added problem of getting up off the floor. When you are a woman past the age of 60, getting up from a prone position flat on the floor is no easy achievement. And so, even the routine procedure of drying my hair has involved me attempting some exceedingly difficult yoga and Pilates moves—moves I might add I have already had to perform each morning in an attempt to get up off my mattress on the floor in the bunk room. And said exercises are not restricted to the day; during the night I must execute certain kick-boxing exercises to try and reach Geoffrey snoring above me in the lower bunk in a futile bid to get him to turn over. We are sleeping foot to foot. I have never yet been able to reach him with a gentle kick-boxing foot prod, he's just that little bit too far away, so instead I hiss: 'Geoffrey, turn over,' throughout the night which has no effect on him whatsoever, but probably makes Ted turn over in his sleep across the landing.

But I must complain no longer. I love this old property; it is charmingly seductive, full of French character. It is in the Maison de Maître-style, (house of the master, that is), the most important house in the village after the grand château up the road. Amanda cheekily changed the name when she bought the property, from House of the Master to House of the Mistress, Maison de Maîtresse. The locals were too polite to ask if she had made a mistake with her French, mistaking *maîtresse* for *maître*. Either she was ignorant of the subtleties of the French language or she meant to announce to the village she was a kept woman. Now they know her, they get her joke. The property was originally owned by a nobleman from Paris who used it as a country retreat. The smaller house, La Petite Maison, was the coach house for the servants and the horses, while the nobleman and his family used the big house.

Steeped in history and redolent of another grand time, the property has already, in my short time here, been responsible for creating some of my most cherished memories, and if I have to do a strenuous yoga and Pilates class each morning to achieve dry and styled hair, and if I find my bosom smeared with a tangy vinaigrette each time I try to get up the stairs and out the front door, then who cares? These are tiny inconveniences compared to the giddy joy of being here with Amanda and all these fascinating people.

Gino has decided to join on the tour and while we originally said we would not take more than eight guests, he is so quiet and unassuming and so obviously still in love with Rosa, we could not refuse him. Rosa has agreed to let him sleep on the day bed in her room. She has not said much about the situation other than that. He follows her around quietly. And as if the poor man has not suffered enough in his romantic quest just to be here near his beloved, he now has a tummy bug. We have all been kind and considerate to him and tried to leave them both alone as much as possible.

After our late lunch yesterday, we watched Maurice, Rosemary and Françoise prepare a Spanish feast of such gustatory excellence we felt we should invite the whole village to partake of it, even the cretins. Maurice sat at the kitchen table in the big house chopping onions, cutting cucumbers and slicing tomatoes all afternoon for Rosemary's gazpacho. Then he shelled prawns, sliced fish, chopped more tomatoes and onions for her seafood extravaganza. Patient and multi-skilled man that he is, he soon had the entire table covered with colourful vegetables, while Rosemary fiddled with the oven and Françoise intervened. At least Luce had returned to Lyon, resulting in one less lively voice in the kitchen.

When the gazpacho came to the table it was served by Ciara who had found her way back to us after going missing for a day. She ladled the cold red soup out carefully into small glasses and looked very charming as she passed it around to the guests. They all loved her; it was the Irish accent, so soft and lilting and when she broke into French, as she often did, it was bewitching. Maurice stood by her at the table and explained the gazpacho's ingredients and preparation method.

'After pureeing all the ingredients and adding soaked bread and paprika, the gazpacho was left to chill for a few hours and ice cubes were added just before serving,' he said, changing from the French teacher of the morning to the maître d of the evening. The Spanish theme had already begun with a couple of glasses of sangria, served from Amanda's giant punch bowl at the table. Amanda looked particularly colourful in a low-cut, hot-pink, tight sweater over a dark skirt. Around her neck hung an enormous silver cross with a large turquoise in its centre. She is fond of overlarge jewellery and it suits her big personality well. She had all the ladies laughing, even though she was just giving them a little talk about sangria. She can make anything sound entertaining. Ted sat quietly watching her, Geoffrey hovered with wine bottles and Gino held on to his aching stomach and looked puzzled.

Rosemary's seafood dish, an epic achievement, contained prawns, tuna and cuttlefish. It resembled *paella*, although it used vermicelli instead of rice as the bulk ingredient.

She made it in a pan so big it took up the entire stove top. We watched her quiet efficient movements as she sautéed large prawns in hot olive oil before removing them and keeping them aside. Then she seared chunks of blood-red tuna and slick white cuttlefish in the prawn-flavoured oil before adding Maurice's chopped tomatoes. She stirred the fish and tomato mixture in the big pan with confident ease, this was obviously a dish she had made many times, and then added generous teaspoons of a rich, red powdered pepper, a pepper she said through her translator Maurice, she had brought with her from Spain as it was the finest in the country. The sizzling pan and the pungent seafood smells made our mouths water as she added the onions. Throughout the demonstration Maurice commentated and translated and my affection for him grew. I had put my complete trust in Amanda when she told me she would organise all the chefs and cooks for our demonstrations. I had never met any of them before and now, here were Rosemary and Maurice, performing like professional television chefs in front of the cameras.

Rosemary now filled the enormous pan right up to the brim with boiling stock she had prepared that afternoon and let it simmer for ten minutes before putting in a whole packet of vermicelli. She then carefully placed the fat prawns in a circular pattern on top of the liquid and it took on a gourmet presentation.

When it was carried carefully to the table by Maurice and Ciara there was such genuine applause and excited exclamations it was as though Brad and Angelina had made an entrance into our little party. When Rosemary arrived a few minutes behind it, she received even louder cheering and clapping. It was another night of inspiring food.

Although we ate with gusto, we had all slowed down on the drinking. It was impossible to keep up the partying pace and after dinner we retired to the kitchen of the small house where Hester and Dean were cleaning up. Ted helped to stack the dishwasher. Ciara disappeared again. There was no singing tonight, our bellies were full and we were all sleepy. Amanda decided to brief us all on the next few days' activities. She brought out her running sheet and went through the planned excursions and activities in detail, even advising us on what to wear. Jessica and Leith wandered in halfway through the briefing and were cross to find they had missed a good opportunity to film.

'You must tell us when you are going to do something like this,' Leith said, drawing me aside discreetly. 'We need time to set up the camera and record. Now you have lost an opportunity. Amanda would have been great to film while addressing the group.'

He made a good point. So far, Amanda, Geoffrey and I had bumbled our way through each day either ignoring the cameras or being too aware of them; the guests had been admirably patient with them, but there had been many times when we had walked in front of cameras spoiling important scenes or not informed Jessica and Leith when we were doing something colourful or exciting. We had certainly recorded some excellent cooking segments, but we had nothing close enough to the enormous amount of footage we would need if Amanda was to realise her dream of becoming the presenter of a lifestyle show.

Leith ordered Geoffrey, Amanda, Jessica and I to sit down right that minute and have a meeting to address this filming problem. There was nowhere to go to talk privately except into the living room, now Jessica and Leith's bedroom. The floor was covered with a large mattress strewn with their tangled camera equipment, suitcases and jumbled piles of clothes. The five of us stepped over the mattress and picked our way over camera bags and wires and tried to sit on the couch where we had stored an upended coffee table and a small side table. Somehow we all managed to seat ourselves awkwardly on the edge of the couch and Leith gave us a stern lecture.

'The five of us need to have a meeting each morning,' he said. 'We need to go over what we will be doing for the day and then we need to plan what part of it we are going to film. So far all we have is a bunch of higgledy-piggeldy home-movie footage which will amount to nothing. Unless we can get structure, this idea of making a lifestyle documentary will not work.' We felt like naughty school-children and promised him we would never give a briefing to the group again without telling him first. We agreed to be organised and plan at the beginning of each day. Geoffrey, Amanda and I would rise early each morning, meet in the kitchen of the small house and have a meeting. Leith would film it. We would then give him a running sheet of what we wanted filmed for the day. We now felt so virtuous we went back to the kitchen to join the others for a last half glass of wine before getting to bed at the reasonable hour of one in the morning.

Today was Wednesday which meant the Uzès markets were running, although not on the frantic and large scale they would on Saturday. However, Wednesday was fresh produce day and after a morning at the market we would meet at Terroir for lunch, a charming restaurant in the Place aux Herbs of Uzès.

The sun was out, the sky a vivid blue, but the lurking Mistral showed no signs of leaving, even though Maurice had declared it might blow itself away today. We arrived at the markets while the stall-holders were still setting up. We watched as bundles of neatly tied asparagus were unloaded from the back of trucks and stacked upright side by side. Large hessian sacks of fresh lavender were set out in front of stalls bearing lavender soaps and oils. Fat, red tomatoes were carefully piled in neat order with their tiny green stems all pointing upwards; multicoloured olives in plastic-lined tubs were positioned on low benches; dried fruits, nuts and lentils were carefully laid out for display in round bowls next to big stainless steel bowls piled high with mountains of freshly made tapenades ranging in colour from deep purple to black, red and green. Thousands of bright-red strawberries, almost the size of pingpong balls, were thrown in red jumbles into wide troughs. The flower merchants lined buckets of roses and lilies in neat rows on the ground alongside punnets of brightly coloured seedlings. It was the start of summer in Uzès and the fresh colours and smells were all around us.

Amanda had decided to stay at home for the morning to deal with her paperwork. The group split up, some in urgent need of strong coffee and others, me, in even more urgent need of purchasing something warm to wear. The market square, surrounded by tall buildings of handsome architecture and dotted with leafy plane trees, was in the shade in the early morning and I was finding the cold intolerable. I waited for the first shop to open and rushed in to buy a thick white sweater on sale for just 19 euros and a singlet to wear close to my body. I put on the layers in the shop's changing room and returned to the streets to stride with Geoffrey around the markets a new warm woman. We watched a jazz trio set up outside one of the cafés and soon their lively music added to the festive market atmosphere. We visited the little *boulangerie*, hidden in the gloom beneath a section of the arcade. The tiny shop had space enough to hold only two or three customers at a time. Baguettes were stacked in neat formation against the wall right up to the ceiling. Bread, still dusty with flour, came in flat, thin loaves and plump round mounds. Rich pastries filled with pork rinds and mushrooms were stacked on the counter.

At this early hour the shop was empty and we could linger over our choices. Later there would be a long line of eager customers snaking back out to the square, never diminishing throughout the morning.

'You can buy something in there and take it to one of the cafés to eat with coffee,' Amanda had told us earlier. 'Most cafés in Uzès do not mind you eating someone else's products if you buy coffee.' This seemed extraordinarily generous to me. I couldn't imagine any café or bistro at home welcoming you in with your bag of buns from the local hot bread shop, but whatever Amanda said was always right, so we purchased rich flaky pastries and took them to the most vibrant of all the cafés where the jazz trio played and boldly sat at the table and opened our bags. Soon Ted wandered in after buying gifts for his wife, followed by Sharon and Margaret, all with their little bags of pastries and we spent a happy hour together in the strengthening sunshine listening to the music, sipping strong coffee and brushing tiny bits of pastry from our lips.

Uzès is a medieval town founded in the fifth century. Today, it is a spectacular Duchy with a reigning Duke and Duchess. Its medieval streets are home to exciting decorator shops, art galleries and dozens of bars and restaurants. Festivals ranging from musical evenings to family days take place most weeks in the summer. The town itself is government protected, so no developer's greed has spoilt its characteristic charm and handsome architecture. It lies at the source of the Ere from where the Roman aqueduct was built in the first century BC. The most famous part of the aqueduct which runs from here to Nîmes, is the Pont du Gard, a place we will be visiting next week when we kayak down the Gardon river.

Between Avignon and Nîmes, Uzès has a population of 10,000. It is an important region for the black truffle; hunters with their truffle dogs have searched the region's woods for centuries to glean this strange and sought-after delicacy.

Amanda told us in late January the truffle festival takes place in the centre of Uzès where sand and small tree branches are trucked in to the centre and fenced off in a pen that is supposed to resemble a little oak forest. Dogs and pigs owned by proud truffle cultivators are brought in to sniff out hidden delicacies placed there. Then to celebrate all things truffle-related, chefs wearing tall white hats make a giant omelette over a fire using 3000 eggs, stirring the omelette with long wooden shovel instruments, and lacing it with shaved truffles.

It's one of the biggest truffle festivals in the region and attracts thousands of visitors. Children as well as adults tuck into the omelette with shouts of appreciation for the intense flavour in these hideously expensive little black truffle diamonds.

Uzès is just one of the towns in France popular with English sea-changers. Their various accents from all areas of the UK can be heard on every street corner, in every shop and all over the market. They buy property, renovate, settle, make other English friends, but many of them have not bothered to learn French.

This shocks Amanda. 'You get so much more out of living here if you speak the language,' she told me when we met her last year. 'Everything is so much easier and the locals respect you for it. A lot of people dream of living in this part of France. I actually followed my dream and made it real. When I first came here I did not have the language but I immediately loved France, the food, the wine, the weather. I liked the people, they are cultured, sophisticated and when you get to know them they are warm and friendly.'

Amanda had not originally planned to live near Uzès. Soon after she arrived in France, she found a little chateau for sale in an area in the hills above Nice, but it was owned by a sheik who did not want to do real estate business with a woman.

'It was run down, but in 60 hectares,' she said. 'I made an offer, but the sheik didn't want to know me. Now I think how fortunate I was. I would have spent all my time worrying about such a large property, how I would run it and make a living from it. It would have needed a lot of work; it was such a big project for one person. I would have been tied to it and had no freedom. Sometimes you are guided by some small thing; fate will steer you towards or away from it and in my case it was a male chauvinist sheik. He did me a big favour by having that attitude.

'I got really serious after the disappointment with the sheik and started looking at properties with my daughter. We must have looked at about 60 properties. We researched, we took photos, we made notes, and in the end we found out not so much what we wanted, but what we didn't want.

'When I found Maison de Maîtresse it felt right straight away. The position was perfect. It is so easy for people to get here. They can fly into Paris, come down on the fast train to Avignon and we are only a 30-minute drive from there. With the sheik's chateau, people would have had to fly into Nice and then drive two and a half hours up in the mountain to find me.

'Maison de Maîtresse was owned by two Swedish families when I bought it. They had been coming to holiday here every year but had a falling out. They wanted to get their money and get out quickly. They were the perfect sellers and I was the perfect buyer. I wanted to be in a village, on a hill, in a stone house with vines growing up the walls, with a swimming pool facing the sun all day. I had not intended to buy two houses joined together but now I am glad I did.'

Amanda has cleverly formed her life where she can live well, indulge in her love of parties and travel while earning a living. When it gets too cold in France at the end of November and when there are no tourists around to rent her accommodation, she packs up and moves back to New Zealand for a few months where she owns an apartment in Auckland, and her family and many friends welcome her to stay in their homes in the north near the Bay of Islands. During the New Zealand summer she indulges in her other passions of diving and boating. And now she has me welcoming her to Australia whenever she feels in the mood to pop over. She certainly has an enviable life.

Now Geoffrey and I wandered the markets, buying cherries, cheese, apricots and baguettes until it was time to meet Amanda at Terroir, not only a restaurant but also a gourmet shop stocking a good selection of olive oils and wines from the area. Amanda knew the owner, Tom, very well, of course. Tom looked French, sounded English, but was actually Swedish and has owned the restaurant for several years; he had reserved a long table for our group outside beneath the dappled shade of a plane tree with a clear view to all the market action.

Geoffrey and I were the first to arrive and to our absolute delight, the Mistral had finally dropped and I could take off the white sweater and sit in the sunshine. Amanda arrived in the mood to celebrate having cleared up all her paperwork. She bustled into the restaurant to speak to Tom. The others all trickled in one by one or in couples, all with stuffed shopping bags bearing the names of many of the stylish little shops in the maze of back lanes and alleyways of Uzès.

As everybody talked excitedly about their morning and showed off their purchases, which varied from stylish clothes to hayfever pills, Tom came out and asked what sort of wine they wanted. 'Any sort,' they replied and so he brought out bottles of red, white and rosé and plonked them down the length of the table. The fun began once again.

We started with octopus salad, aubergine dip, artichoke hearts with basil, goat cheese with olive oil and Provençal herbs. Between us we ordered almost every item on the menu: carpaccio of scallops with grapefruit juice and roquette salad; foie gras with smoked duck breast and green salad, and many *tartines grillées*, open sandwiches. There is something so fresh about French grilled sandwiches, especially the tasty *croque monsieur*, that delicious thick sandwich filled with ham and topped with gruyère cheese on the outside before being grilled so the cheese melts and drips down the sides. Every French café will sell you its own version of the *croque monsieur*, some coated in a mornay or *béchamel* sauce, mostly served with a green salad. The *croque madame*, another French special which originated as a fast food in small French cafés, is also filled with ham and topped with melted gruyère cheese but with a fried egg on top. I have tried to make both these sandwiches at home, and although I've had success, they never taste as good as they do in France.

Tom's *tartines grillées* were filled with a variety of delicious ingredients: cod brandade; eggplant, tomatoes, zucchini and parmesan; sun-dried tomato with mozzarella and basil; goat cheese, cured ham and *tapenade*; anchovy paste, pickled onions, spices and olives. A little pile of lightly dressed salad sat by their side, and as we ate and drank in the now warm sunshine, a feeling of extraordinary contentment came over all of us.

'I have to pinch myself,' Eve said as she dug her fork into a mound of goat cheese and looked out over the market, now winding down as everyone headed home to prepare lunch with their market purchases. The Mistral had completely disappeared and it was difficult to even remember feeling cold. 'I feel so fortunate,' Eve continued. 'Did my husband really leave me after 35 years of marriage? It could have been the best thing he'd ever done.'

I felt so happy for her, I picked up a corkscrew lying on the table and told her to hold it up. I took a photo of her with the coil of the corkscrew pointing up to the Provence sunshine. With the colourful food on the table and the glorious architecture of Uzès as a backdrop she looked young and happy and very lovely.

'Send that to your husband,' I said. 'With the message, "screw you".'

8

The Myth of the Rude French

We have found the French people to be charming and friendly, even though we have almost gone out of our way to look for a rude person. Admittedly the only French people we have met so far have been Amanda's friends and therefore welcoming and friendly but even during our few days in Paris before arriving at St. Maximin we did not find a rude person, not even a surly waiter. Every restaurant in Paris seemed to employ only friendly waiters who loved us. They were all happy to speak English, especially after we first offered a *'Je suis désolée, mais je ne parle pas français.'* All this talk of rude French people appeared to be a myth to us, although we had encountered a certain French stubbornness.

The day before our tour started, Amanda, Geoffrey and I had visited a large discount supply store for all the basic items we would need, including tins of olives, wheels of cheese, bottles of vinegar and jams, trays of yogurts, commercial-sized packets of serviettes and butter.

It had been a typically hot Provence June day, well before that annoying Mistral had arrived, and I had worn only a singlet top and a light skirt. When we walked into the vast and sprawling store we discovered it was in fact a giant cold room.

'The management will provide you with warm jackets,' Amanda said as we stepped inside and received a blast of icy air. I immediately made a dash for a counter at the front to ask a woman for assistance. She herself was snug beneath a long, thick yellow coat reaching down to her knees. I asked her for a coat.

'*Non*,' she replied. 'All the coats are out.' She motioned towards a group of shoppers wearing the same thick yellow coats pushing trolleys the size of semi-trailers around wide aisles of goods stacked high to the roof. 'We already have other customers over there wearing them. When they finish their shopping and return their coats, then you shall have a coat.'

Her attitude was so final I did not dare point out there was a spare coat hanging over the back of an empty chair right next to her, obviously used by a staff member who was not on duty. I slunk off and joined Amanda and Geoffrey shivering and now pushing their own semi-trailer sized trolley into a large separate cheese room. I followed them inside where the temperature was even colder. I very much wanted to inspect the cheeses; there were endless varieties in giant rounds, enormous slabs and truck-tyre size wheels, ranging from roquefort through to cheddar, gruyère, brie and camembert, but I was so shaking with cold, I could not relax enough for even a cursory look. Geoffrey and Amanda who wore more clothing than I, were shivering and hugging their arms around their bodies but determined to shop and get this important chore done.

I hurried back out of the cheese room and approached the woman at the counter again. '*Excusez-moi*,' I said very politely. 'I know you said there were no more coats, but there is a spare one hanging over that chair. Could I borrow that? I will return it immediately I have finished shopping.'

She looked at me as though I was a hearing-challenged person. '*Non*,' she said. 'That is for the staff. It is not allowed.'

'But there is no staff member using it,' I said reasonably, hugging my body and shivering dramatically to further make my point. She was not moved. '*Non*, it is not permitted to give out the coats of the staff,' she snapped, turning to her paperwork. I slunk off again feeling stupid and freezing and thwarted. I tried to concentrate on the shopping for another 10 icy minutes, following a shivering Amanda and Geoffrey around with their trolley, shakily loading bags of sugar and bulk containers of tea and coffee into the trolley but it really was like being trapped inside a fridge in your underwear.

Back to the reception counter I returned. 'Please,' I pleaded with the woman. 'You really must lend me that coat. It is completely wrong that you have a spare coat here hanging idly over the back of a chair when you can see how cold I am. I cannot concentrate on the shopping and I plan to spend a great deal of money in here. Please, I beg you, give me the coat.'

This time she looked at me as if I was a cockroach she'd suddenly found in her steaming bowl of bouillabaisse. *'Non,'* she replied and turned away.

I went next to one of the cashiers, snug and warm in her own yellow coat with—the *outrage* of it—yet another coat slung over the back of her chair. (Cashiers all sit on chairs in French supermarkets, very practical and comfortable.)

'See that woman over there,' I said, pointing to the first woman once I'd established the cashier spoke English. 'She has a spare coat on the chair and she won't let me borrow it.' By now I was blue with cold, little icicles were about to form on the end of my nose, my nipples were alert and my teeth where chattering so loudly I could barely speak.

'It is not permitted for her to give you that coat,' the second woman said and turned her head away.

'Okay,' I said. 'Then perhaps I can have the coat on the back of your own chair. You already have one on and you seem to be warm enough.'

'*Non,*' she replied and bent over her cash register.

By now I was angry. I returned to the first woman and said: 'I am asking you one last time to let me borrow that coat. I am freezing my tits off here.' I used my best Aussie twang and the colloquial expression convinced it would soften her.

It didn't. '*Non,*' she said and returned to her work.

No-one had been very rude to me, just dismissive and unhelpful. There was a certain French attitude going on here, unspoken but clear, that said: 'I am not going to bend a rule for you even if you are a customer spending 800 euros and one with a blue face, big nipples and chattering teeth. I am in control of spare coats here and there is nothing you can do about it. So pee off and freeze your Australian tits off for all I care. It's a vulgar expression anyway.'

The year before we had encountered a similar attitude at a tiny railway station in a small village in south-west France where a cute yellow train chuffs tourists on a scenic ride high up into the mountains. We had arrived at the village at midday, well before the train was due to leave at 1.30pm and had gone to the station to purchase our tickets to ensure no last-minute rush.

'You cannot buy tickets until 1.15pm,' the man behind the ticket counter informed us.

It seemed ridiculous. He was there, we were there. Why not sell us a ticket and get rid of us?

'But wouldn't it save time if we bought tickets now?' we asked politely. 'Then we can be out of your way.'

'*Non*, you must come back at 1.15pm,' he said and walked away from his little window.

We left the station and found a café in the village and ate steak and *pommes frites* and returned at 12.45pm to see if we might buy our tickets.

'*Non*,' the same man said and walked away from his window again.

When we returned yet again at 1pm there was a queue winding its way out of the station, through the car park and out onto the road. There was no-one at the ticket window.

'What is this?' we said and joined the end of the long queue. 'They will never be able to sell tickets to this many people in 15 minutes.'

And neither they could. When the ticket box opened at 1.15pm, we waited and tutted and fumed and stood for many long minutes; the queue shuffled along unbearably slowly, each passenger in front of us seeming to have endless questions before he could actually make a ticket purchase. At 1.29pm people were panicking that they would miss the train.

They called out questions in French to those at the front of the queue who shouted something back but did not hurry over their ticket purchases. The train guard came in and shouted something, obviously to tell everyone to hurry up as the train was due to leave. A few people actually left the queue to get on the train without a ticket, and with our hearts ticking with the quick heartbeat you experience when you are about to miss a train, we made it to the front and finally bought our tickets just as the train's whistle was blowing and it was about to pull out of the station.

'We could have bought the bloody tickets an hour ago,' I shouted to Geoffrey as we ran and leapt Tom Cruise-like, on to the departing train.

But these are our only encounters with a stubborn French attitude. Apart from those two incidents, I have found the French helpful and agreeable, and funnily, all but the woman in the discount store seem to get my Australian humour.

After we'd returned from our long lunch in Uzès, Amanda decided she simply must have a rest. She put on her blue bikini bottom and stretched out on a sunbed with her brown breasts to the sun. Ted busied himself with the washing and ironing and within five minutes had a series of washing-machine related questions for Amanda. She had only just closed her eyes and I could see she was irritated.

'I really need to have a rest,' she said after she'd satisfied Ted's washing machine queries, but within a few moments more, someone had asked if they could use the internet which required her getting up again, unlocking the bars to her bedroom to get to her tiny office. As soon as she had done this and set herself out again in the sun, someone else had another question for her, and so it went for the rest of the afternoon. I had not even sat down.

'I only want an hour to myself,' Amanda said crossly, peeling herself up off the chair one more time and giving up all thoughts of rest.

'You are a tour leader,' I reminded her. 'Tour leaders cannot lie down with their boobies in the air expecting to snooze or sunbathe.' I was pleased to note I wasn't the only one finding tour leading such a challenge.

In the late afternoon, Christian, another of our guest chefs, arrived with a large ice-box and a basket of red and green capsicum, cucumbers, celery and zucchini.

He brought an entourage of two with him: his partner Pierre and Joanne the attractive, chestnut-haired English lady who had cooked for us on day two of our tour. A placid and gentle gay French man, Christian was going to cook his specialty, a dish he called 'drunken quail on the sofa.' It comprised quail, cooked in a ginger and wine sauce, sitting on squares of thick toasted bread, their little sofas.

His impeccable manners and soft charm had an immediate winning effect on everyone and into the kitchen we went to watch him at work. He had brought the tiny quails plucked and ready to be cooked, but still with their beaky little heads attached. Watching him cut *la tête* off each of the minuscule birds was almost as gruesome for some as eating the frogs' legs.

'Normally, I would serve them with the heads on,' Christian said through Joanne his interpreter. 'That is the way we eat them, but for you Australians, I don't think it is so good.'

It wasn't so good. We would have preferred not to have seen their little heads, let alone watched them being chopped off. We like to distance ourselves from the farmer and prefer to view only the finished product, wrapped and clean in the supermarket or sitting prettily in a butcher's window. But here in the country, where people often bought directly from the farmer, little parts of creatures you would rather not see were there, whole and intact. We were to see this again when Françoise prepared her *coq au vin* dinner. She came into the kitchen with the cockerel pieces she had bought from the farmer down the road, proudly showing us the cockerel's two white testicles, before whipping them off with a sharp knife.

Christian browned the headless quails in a frying pan with hot olive oil, their little tummies fat against their scrawny legs. He then peeled and thinly sliced six thick ginger roots before placing the browned quails into a large black casserole dish and tumbling the ginger matchsticks over them. With a happy call of *voilà*, he poured the contents of a whole bottle of white wine over them.

'This is a special wine,' he announced holding the bottle up for the camera. 'It is an aged wine, very strong, very pungent, very good for you.'

Then he opened another bottle and poured most of it into the pan with another cry of *voilà*.

'Two bottles of wine?' I asked, aghast. It appeared a lot, even to an old lush like me.

'Yes,' he replied. 'This is why this dish is called "drunken quail on the sofa". The quail must swim in the wine.' He poured a glass for himself.

There was another happy *voilà* as he placed the dish on top of the stove to simmer, before turning his attention to the salad.

'Because the quail is such a rich dish, I will serve a simple salad before it,' he announced.

He cut the capsicum into thin strips and then into tiny cubes and diced the celery before cutting the tomatoes into neat wedges and adding everything to frisee lettuce. He dressed it in the bowl, pouring olive oil over the ingredients, then adding a generous sprinkling of sea salt. Next, a swirl of balsamic vinegar, a grind of black pepper and then a vigorous tossing before a tasting. A declaration of 'more salt', another vigorous tossing, another taste, a final *voilà* and the salad was pronounced satisfactory.

A check of the simmering quails assured him all was okay on top of the stove and he then gave his attention to the zucchini, cutting them into neat circles and placing them in a circular pattern in an ovenproof dish.

'I will make a zucchini gratin to accompany the quails,' he said. 'It is also very rich.'

He cracked 12 eggs into a bowl and gave them a good whisk with a fork and added two large tubs of crème fraîche. After a grind of pepper and a sprinkling of sea salt the mixture was poured over the zucchini. Into the oven it went with several shouts of *voilà* and a final inspection of the oven knob.

'This is not my kitchen so I must be careful with the oven temperature,' he said.

'I still have not managed to turn it on,' I told him.

He then boiled tiny speckled quail eggs. So small, like marbles, and beautifully speckled, they were cooked for four minutes. After cooling them in cold water he carefully peeled away the little shells.

It had all been slow work with many stops for the camera and with Joanne interpreting for him. None of these chefs had appeared before a camera before and they were all brave and patient.

By the time the drunken quails came out on a silver platter sitting on their bread sofa beds drenched in the wine and ginger sauce and dotted with the little white quail eggs, it was very late. Amanda had put on her Pink Martini album and the music was sexy, the night air warm. Night time under the pergola in the walled garden is especially romantic; the grape vines and geraniums take on an extra magic in the evening light and the flickering candles flatter everyone. The quails were moist, the flesh melting off their little bones on to the alcoholic sofa beds.

Maurice and Françoise had taken the evening off and gone with Hester to the café in the village and for the first time it was just our group at the table. The evening drifted on languidly until midnight, when Christian's partner, Pierre, a Greek man with a voice much like Pavarotti's we had been told, was encouraged to sing.

Shy and quiet, he said he would prefer not to. We insisted and what could he do but give in in the face of nine strong women. His big voice boomed out into the warm night while we all sat enchanted. As I listened to him sing I thought how fortunate we were to be treated to so much local entertainment, and on such a personal level. Had there ever been another tour that provided so much? Had another tour ever given its guests a variety of music, so many epicurean experiences, such a line-up of talented chefs, such exciting personally escorted tours? And the answer is, quite frankly, no. I had been on the internet and visited travel agents to check out other Provence tours before we left, and while almost all of them provided an excellent Provence experience and introductions to local foods and wines and meanders around medieval villages, none of them had offered as many different chef presentations or such an intimate and relaxed experience.

I doubt there is another tour leader in the world who would offer her guests unlimited access to wine, not to mention the occasional swig from her own duty-free vodka bottle, and be willing to share her gentlemanly husband with her guests, indeed offer him with her good wishes so he could serve their drinks, and be used as a dance partner, chauffeur, guide and bodyguard.

Good manners come naturally to Geoffrey and he never once let any of the guests want for anything. He ensured the van was always parked as close as possible to our destination so they would never have far to walk, often having to drive back 15 minutes down the road to find a park and walk back. Rarely did any of them have to top up a glass of wine. And never in the history of all tours, had guests been given such free and intimate access to their host's property ... or been exposed so often to their host's titties.

Our guests all felt free to use the washing machine at their will and take out the ironing board at their leisure (when Ted wasn't using it). They trooped in to Amanda's bedroom to reach her tiny office; they had been privy to many of her secrets, worn some of her wardrobe and generally had access to her home as though it was their own. They had met many of her friends and been accepted by them all. I felt very proud to have brought this group here and introduced them to Amanda, and I knew that, like my own, their lives would be richer for knowing her. And that's enough self-promotion.

At one in the morning when everyone was feeling sleepy after another multi-course dinner, something was brought to Amanda's attention that displeased her immensely. Ciara, our charming but often absent Irish kitchen-hand had to be taken into Avignon early in the morning for another of her exam commitments. Hester had somehow been roped and had agreed to drive Ciara into town at 6am. A helpful and innocent enough arrangement. Unfortunately it coincided with a visit from some insurance inspectors coming to look at roof damage at Ab Fab. Amanda was convinced Hester would not be back in time from Avignon to meet them.

'We made this arrangement with the insurance inspectors months ago,' Amanda said angrily when she found out Hester would be missing from the property early in the morning, and missing because of Ciara.

'We will never get the insurance inspectors to come out again, it could take a year,' she cried in anger and immediately started making calls on her mobile phone.

'Can we take Ciara into Avignon?' I suggested.

'No, we have to be ready early to take the tour guests to Les Baux-de-Provence,' she said. 'We can't keep them waiting.'

Indeed we could not, especially to run around for an employee who had not exactly been as efficient, punctual or dutiful as we would have wished.

Amanda's small fume quickly turned into a large rant. The delicious drunken quails and the dramatic opera singing were all forgotten as she punched numbers into her phone trying to find Hester and Ciara. Geoffrey and I made soothing noises and tried helpful suggestions, all useless.

'Surely there has to be another way to get Ciara to Avignon without involving Hester,' we said.

This only caused her further anger. 'No,' she snapped. 'I don't know why Hester agreed to take her; she must have known she'd never get back in time. It took so long to get these insurance inspectors to come out. We may never be able to get them back here again.'

'You've already said that,' I said. 'Let's think of a solution.'

'There is none.'

Around and around the problem Amanda went until one by one the guests departed for bed.

'Let's not embarrass Christian,' I said quietly to Amanda, who was now on the verge of a small breakdown. Christian looked happy enough; the French are used to such fiery displays of temper I believe.

But dear Amanda could not be placated. She had worked herself into a frenzy and somehow, God knows how, word of her anger travelled out of Maison de Maîtresse and down the cobbled road to Hester in the village café at 1.30 in the morning. She arrived, concerned that Amanda was so upset because of her offer to assist Ciara. She was followed by Maurice and Françoise. There ensued much confused babbling, then an unacceptable raising of voices. We all tried to placate Amanda and calm her down but she was having none of it.

Her anger was not directed at Hester, it was directed fully at Ciara. This girl was supposed to have been a help to us in our quest to be the best tour leaders in the world, but here she was causing inconvenience and trouble.

Hester told Amanda she would be back in plenty of time to meet the insurance inspectors, I told Amanda Hester would be back in plenty of time to meet the insurance inspectors, Geoffrey, Maurice and Françoise told Amanda Hester would be back in plenty of time to meet the insurance inspectors, but still Amanda could not be pacified. There was nothing more I could do to calm Amanda, so I too went off to bed.

As I brushed my teeth in the upstairs bathroom, Amanda's angry voice and repeated cussing wafted up through the window. If I could hear her so clearly, so too could our guests. It could not continue. Down the three flights of stairs I ran, out into the garden, toothbrush in hand, white foam frothing at my mouth. I shouted: 'Shut up!' spitting toothpaste all down my front, whereupon Amanda looked startled for a moment, took another gulp of her wine, and then actually did shut up. Both houses finally went quiet for the night.

9
Venice in a Quarry

In the morning, Amanda was contrite. She apologised to every guest personally, apologised to Hester, Maurice and François and Geoffrey and then apologised to me.

Her apology was accepted with alacrity and warmth by everyone and we all continued on happily. We never did find out if Hester took Ciara to Avignon and got back in time. We never did find out if the insurance inspectors had arrived. We never did find out why indeed there was roof damage at Ab Fab. In the light of another day full of expectation and promise, we had moved on quickly and forgotten all about Ciara and insurance inspectors before the last batch of croissants had been put in the oven.

We were all looking forward to another long day out touring the ancient castle ruins of Les Baux-de-Provence and then lunching at one of the region's most renowned restaurants. Les Baux-de-Provence is a 40-minute drive from St. Maximin through vine and forest country and we set off in our usual convoy. Hester, who was joining us for part of the day, came in the car with Françoise, Maurice and I. We were behind the blue van with Geoffrey and the guests. Gino and Rosa went in Gino's hired car. Jessica and Leith came behind, squashed in the back seat of Amanda's sports car.

Even though it was a relatively short drive, there was much telephoning between cars to ensure we kept in each other's sights. I don't know why we hadn't arranged to meet in the car park at the entrance to Les Baux-de-Provence; it sounds like a much simpler idea now that I am back home and have full control of my thoughts once more.

Being a tour guide is so much harder than it sounds, even when you have a group of the best behaved guests God ever put together. The corralling of people before each outing is a difficult endeavour, and it doesn't get any easier with each day. The minute I have them all outside the house ready to go, someone decides she simply must go back for a jacket. This prompts another who says she absolutely cannot go without her scarf, something she thought she had put in her bag, but hadn't. When two have gone back inside the house, someone else suddenly remembers a missing camera, another requires a last loo visit, and by then, Amanda, who is loathe to waste a precious minute waiting for anything wanders around the corner to make a telephone call, to indulge in some dirty talk with one of her lovers.

Speaking of which, the lover with the truck has gone strangely quiet, probably word has reached him that Amanda is busy with a tour group, but *Chocolat* has been on the telephone and email daily. He is desolate that he cannot be here with us and has made constant inquiries about Amanda's progress as a tour guide, followed by pleading inquiries as to her fidelity.

'*Tu es sage et fidèle?*' are you behaving and faithful? he asks her on the phone, obviously a French expression used between lovers, to which Amanda replies an emphatic '*oui, oui*' without even a blush. *Chocolat* is becoming serious about Amanda, something she has not encouraged. She does not want commitment from any of her men, other than that to service her regularly and in a suitably energetic manner.

Now it appears *Chocolat* has fallen in love with her, and while she is very fond of him, and especially enamoured of his sexual dexterity, she wants it to go no further.

But what has all this got to do with Les Baux-de-Provence, I hear you wonder? Absolutely nothing, I just thought it might amuse you. Amanda has given me her permission and blessing to write what I like about her, a display of generosity that overwhelms me, and one that few writers could ever hope to have presented to them.

Les Baux-de-Provence is a commune and a small village enjoying a spectacular position in the Alpilles Mountains. It sits on the crest of a rocky outcrop and is topped by a ruined castle. To get to the top you must walk up through a narrow winding street flanked by shops and cafés. During our briefing the night before Amanda had warned everyone not to be seduced by the shops until we had finished touring the castle ruins.

'You will have time on the way down to visit the shops,' she warned, giving them a stern look. 'Please let us try and stick together until we reach the top. Up there you will be given headphones that will give you the history of the castle as you walk around the ruins.' It was a monumental challenge to get everyone to do just that, one that required me rounding them up like a sheepdog every time one of them pointed her nose in the direction of a brightly displayed shop. Yet, somehow we managed to get them all to the top and as we ushered them into the little office to get our tickets to the castle ruins, a simple enough task, two of them dashed off to a shop and Amanda disappeared to make yet another telephone call. After more rounding up and some stern words given as gently as I could, I had them all inside the office once again, where a little chaos ensued.

This tour was to take place in two parts. The first, in this ruined castle; the second, down the bottom, once we had yet again traversed the siren-like lure of the shops, in the Cathédrale d'Images, a vast underground quarry where stunning exhibitions are staged. Enormous images are displayed on the quarry walls accompanied by appropriate music, and Amanda had promised us a visual treat—an exploration of Venice—that would take our breath away.

So, while Geoffrey attempted to buy group tickets for the Les Baux castle and the Cathédrale d'Images experiences, two of the guests went through the turnstile too quickly with only one of the tickets. It sounds like a silly little oversight now, but it caused consternation in the small ticket office. A queue of tourists had formed outside behind our group; people were getting annoyed at us congesting the ticket booth; Amanda finished her telephone call and attempted to rectify the situation with her excellent French; the ticket clerks got irritated at our stupidity; I became agitated, Geoffrey became frustrated, the guests became bored and showed signs of wandering off again.

'We can't even buy tickets without confusion,' I said to Geoffrey once we had resolved the problem and finally herded everyone through the turnstiles with their proper tickets. 'I've been thinking that we are the best tour leaders in the world, now I'm not so sure. What kind of tour leaders are we?'

'Good ones,' he replied placatingly. 'What's a little fuss over ticket buying? It happens all the time. Just relax; it's nothing.'

Before we broke up from the group to explore the castle ruins on our own, we stopped by an enormous wooden catapult, a massive construction with a long pole from which dangled a menacing leather slinging saddle. A young man dressed in ancient costume was giving a demonstration.

'We must watch this; everybody, stay,' I ordered as they were about to take off. We all scrambled for a seat on a long wooden viewing bench and listened to the young man.

The protective hilltop position meant Les Baux was settled very early in human history. When you built anything thousands of years ago, a hilltop position was always number one on the location list. You could see your enemies coming long before they arrived, giving you plenty of time to pop on the vat and have boiling oil to pour on them and start up the catapult to sling something fearsome at them. Evidence of human habitation has been found at Les Baux dating back as far as 6000BC which is a very, very long time ago. During the Middle Ages it was the seat of a powerful feudal lordship controlling 79 towns and villages. The Lords of Baux controlled Provence for many years.

The young man talked in an animated fashion, mostly in French, although his English was perfect, enticing us with dynamic arm-waving at the catapult before calling for volunteers to swing the big leather saddle that would send an object flying through the air … I think it was a basket ball. Two of our group ran to be involved and stood by with anticipation, but after another ten minutes of excited talking and arranging the volunteers by the side of the catapult, moving them to the other side, changing them back again, some more frantic talk, a bit of shouting for added drama, another volunteer manoeuvre, there was still no catapult action. Everyone became bored.

'Why the heck doesn't he let them shoot the thing?' we said to each other, shuffling our bottoms restlessly on the bench, before the young man continued talking for another ten drawn out minutes. Finally, he swung the leather saddle back a short distance and the ball dribbled out. It was such an anticlimax we all laughed and felt stupid, and then split up and went off to explore. Had we been there centuries ago we might have seen a similarly dressed young man with a crew of 60 firing two 100 kilo stones an hour up to

200 metres—that's what the catapult was capable of, and did on a daily basis during feuding times. You can understand now why the authorities at Les Baux allow only a young man dressed in costume to dribble a basket ball from it.

Geoffrey and I have never experienced much success working tourist headphones. The idea is to proceed methodically from point to point, press a button on the headset to hear the history of that point. Make one mistake or miss one of the stops and you are out of sync with the headphones. So it was that we went from point to point, scrambling over the rocks, fiddling with the headphones, finding either the voice talking to us about the point we had left three stops before or no voice at all. So instead, we read the information boards at each site which were informative and written in English as well as French.

We stopped at a sinister solid wooden battering ram the size of a small rocket. There was no young man demonstrating its powerful use here but it was easy to imagine it being swung by a team of muscular young men trying to knock down unyielding castle gates. As we looked at these primeval and barbaric weapons it was impossible not to think about the sophisticated weapons of today and shudder at the thought that man has been trying to perfect ways to kill other men for thousands of years. We rushed on at the awful thought to scramble over more ruins and read information boards at less sinister sites. The Provence Lords, strong though they were, were deposed in the twelfth century, but the great castle became renowned for its court and culture. Now, the ruins provide just a hint of what had taken place there, but if you are of a creative mind to picture scenes of grand lords lording and commoners commoning during the Middle Ages then you would love peeking through large cracks in old stone walls, walking up steep stone steps and down into small dungeons.

Les Baux was granted to the Grimaldi family, rulers of Monaco, in 1642. To this day the title of Marquis des Baux remains with the Grimaldis, although administratively the town is French. In 1822 bauxite was discovered here, a mineral that was mined extensively in the area until the last century when it ran out. It is these bauxite quarries that are now the home of Cathédrale d'Images.

Geoffrey and I met up with Amanda, near a set of stocks and after we'd all put our heads in them for photos, we scrambled over rocks and climbed steep stone steps to the very top of the ruins where we stood for a long time taking in the view out to Aix-en-Provence, Mont Sainte-Victoire, Marseille, Arles and the Camargue.

Just below the castle, the landscape consisted of thousands of stubby grey rocks poking up in twisted and gnarled formations. This weird view of dramatic rocks and cliffs was said to be the inspiration for Dante Alighieri's vision of hell in his *Divine Comedy*.

On the way back, we stopped in the tiny church just near the ticket office. Inside, pictures of paintings of the area by famous impressionist artists were shown on the wall in slide-show form. A scene of a Provence field by Cézanne lingered on the screen for moments before being melded with a recent photograph of a similar scene. All this happened to a cello accompaniment. Many visitors find this little church and the lovely slide show the perfect respite after scrambling over the ruins on a hot day.

We made our way down; the others all strolled down at their leisure, stopping at the many shops to buy jewellery, trinkets, souvenirs. Les Baux is now completely taken over by the tourist trade and with its historic value it receives thousands of visitors each day in the summer. Its present resident population in the village is just 22 and most of the buildings are no more than evocative ruins.

When we were finally a group again, meeting in the car park and showing off small purchases, we filed down to the Cathédrale d'Images for the exhibition of Venetian pictures. As we walked into the wide and lofty quarry corridor surrounded by looming stone walls, the images began below our feet. We were walking into Venice on shimmering water with spine-tingling operatic music all around us. The effect was dizzying and we clutched each other for support and continued to walk on water into the quarry cathedral as gondolas glided by us on the stone walls. It was so wonderful we were all speechless. Just writing about it now makes the hairs on my arms stand up. We explored the splendour of Venice, our senses alive with the changing images on the walls and the soaring music. Above us were the overhanging balconies and shuttered windows of Venice, around us the mysterious alleyways, magnificent squares and romantic bridges. We peeked through porticos and went inside churches to gaze in wonder at the frescos of Titian and Tintoretto. It was the kind of reverent experience that requires no speaking.

We split up and wandered silently. Alongside the Grand Canal we walked, Geoffrey and I clutching each other to prevent swaying as the images danced and fluttered all around us. Out into St Mark's Square we came, to the Doge's Palace, that supreme symbol of Venice, and all the while the stirring music filled our heads.

We found Amanda, staggering around in the dark on her own, her eyes up to the walls.

'Hold on to us,' we said, and Geoffrey took her under one arm, me under the other, and the three of us tottered around the quarry in an almost hypnotic state. Inside Venetian villas we strolled and then finally, off to Venice's famous *Carnevale* opera. We glided around the sumptuous Venetian galleries and mingled with the beautiful masked people on the walls as Verdi serenaded us in the background.

Finally we strolled into the Venetian night where water melded with the sky and it all became a mirror of fragile beauty. After a long while we staggered out of the quarry into the daylight, silent and overwhelmed.

The Cathédrale d'Images exists because a man called Albert Plecy—and we love him very much for his vision—thought it a good idea to use the old quarries to stage exhibitions. 'Our forefathers took centuries to build cathedrals from stone,' he told us through a statement in a glossy brochure bought at the gift shop. 'Our Cathédrals of Images can be put up in a second.' I think it might have taken more than a second to organise the pictures, the music and the technology to make the images change and dance, but I understood what Albert meant.

We met Hester outside and waited silently with her for the others to come out. We were interested to see their reactions and as we guessed, each guest emerged into the daylight in the same emotional state as we had. It was some time before we returned to normal speech.

Amanda had made reservations for lunch at a restaurant called Le Paradou, a 15-minute drive from Les Baux. 'If we are not there at precisely 1pm we will lose our reservation,' she told us the night before. 'It is one of the most difficult restaurants to get into and they have impressed upon me, the importance of being on time.'

Naturally, this put me in a state of nerves. How was I going to round up the group and get them from Les Baux to Le Paradou on time? I fussed around them, demanding they hurry out of the gift shop, fluttered annoyingly over each one of them and finally pushed their backsides into the van and we arrived precisely on time at Le Paradou, an unassuming white building on a main road, in the middle of nowhere. I wondered what all the reservation nonsense was about.

I have friends who yearned to experience Gordon Ramsay's London restaurant when they visited the UK. They had to use contacts and influences before they left Australia months before to secure a reservation and when they did, the rules and requirements for visiting were overwhelming. They had to fill out forms, email their bank account number, give evidence of their life savings, re-mortgage their house, send a deposit of one hundred pounds, sell their souls and offer up their first-born as a guarantee they would be on time. If they were even 15 minutes late, they were told, their table would not be available to them, neither would their one hundred pound deposit. I remember scoffing at them. Who would want to visit such a pretentious place, I asked them and they answered 'we do' and when they returned to Australia, they said it was worth every bit of the $A700 it cost for the two of them.

However, Gordon Ramsay is a celebrity chef and whether you love or hate him you have to concede he can make ridiculous demands simply because he can. It was difficult to understand how an unassuming restaurant in rural France could have a similar attitude, but obviously it could. Le Paradou has been written about in gastronomic magazines and people were prepared to travel far for its renowned culinary fare. When we arrived, we found an empty giant tour bus at its door. There are few things more off-putting for a traveller than to arrive at any highlight, especially a restaurant, just after a big bus has disgorged a large tour group. (Our small and well-mannered group does not count.) This enormous bus could hold at least 100 people and obviously all of them were inside Le Paradou. We opened the restaurant doors with trepidation. We were right to be nervous. Apart from one empty table, the restaurant was packed and loud from the tour group, and, worse … it was an American tour group. Now, I love Americans, I really do, I have written a book about California, that's how much I love them. I find Americans charming and delightful, but Americans holidaying in

Europe are quite a challenge: their loudness, their ignorance of all things outside their own country, their reluctance to even attempt a foreign word, their demands for cheeseburgers and Coke ... it's irritating, annoying ... you know what I mean. This group was from Alabama, all members of the same tennis club we were to find out later, and had finished their starters and were on the way to their main courses. When our group was settled at the spare table and given a glass of wine, I approached the kitchen.

'You will be serving us soon, won't you?' I said as calmly as I could once I'd established that they understood and could speak English. I had a fear of our group being kept waiting for hours until the American group had been served. A calm reassurance was given. 'It is a set menu, *Madame*. It is all prepared.' But I was still not convinced, so I did what I always do when I am stressed, got heavily stuck into the wine.

Everyone in our group immediately relaxed. The Americans were giving the restaurant a lively buzz and there was an atmosphere of fun. Touring Americans are the friendliest people on earth; already one of them, a woman in her 60s, had approached our table to ask where we were from. Ted took on the role of spokesperson.

'Australia,' he told her.

'Where is that?' she replied sincerely. 'Near Proveraurnce or whatever you call this place we're at right now?'

'Provence,' we corrected her and informed her Australia was not close by. But she was not interested in correct pronunciations let alone a lesson in geography. She had an exaggerated southern drawl and her ignorance was so profound it was beautiful. She draped herself over Ted and continued chatting amiably.

'We are touring all over France,' she said. 'We've come from Cannery today.'

'Er, Cannery, where's that?' we asked.

'Cannery, that place where they have the famous film festival every year,' she replied and we laughed at her which she interpreted as a friendly laugh and went to lean over Maurice, talking inanely until our entrees arrived and she wandered back to her own group.

The wine was flowing freely at our table and within 15 minutes, our own numbers had risen to 20 with the addition of an Englishman, a friend of Amanda's who lived nearby whom she had summonsed by telephone.

Le Paradou was very French with an imposing wooden bar running the length of the room. Stone walls and wooden beams gave it a dark and warm ambience and we all relaxed and ate our eggplant and asparagus salads. It was beautiful food, served without fuss, the produce allowed to star.

'Why is it the salads taste so much better here?' I asked Amanda.

'It's the vinaigrette,' she replied. 'The French use a four-to-one ratio rather than three-to-one as we do, four parts olive oil, one vinegar. And they use only the best Dijon mustard.'

Over lamb with a potato mash and a whole head of roasted garlic, a sense of exceptional wellbeing crept over us all again. The bread as well as the wine, was coming out in generous quantities.

Bread is always complimentary in France and you are encouraged to ask for more as you run out. It is often used to mop up between courses at a particularly long meal, where the one plate will stay in front of you and be used for each course having been wiped immaculately clean by your good self with the bread.

Jessica and Leith were filming us eating and laughing, and the lady from Alabama was highly intrigued. She returned to our group and placed her elbows on the table with her bottom stuck up in the air.

'What are y'all filming here?' she asked. Ted told her we were famous Australian television celebrities. She ran back to her group to pass on this bit of exciting information and they all looked across at us with shining eyes. It appeared these Americans were all friends who toured three or four times every year. One of the members was an excellent organiser and gathered them annually for whirlwind tours. She organised a tour guide to meet them in Europe and take over. Amanda sought out the tour guide now and brought her over to me. She said she was stationed in Paris and told us she found it easy to move large tour groups around Europe. This American group was to visit 20 places in a few days; even today they were to get back on the bus after the large lunch and go on to Avignon and Nîmes. 'How do you do it?' I asked her in complete admiration.

She shrugged. 'It's easy; these people are very good.'

We looked at the Americans, eating, drinking, talking loudly, completely relaxed. 'They will all get on the bus and sleep,' she said confidently. 'They're good.'

After large plates of cheese had done the rounds of the restaurant several times and we all had our fill of brie, camembert and strong goat cheese, Ted approached the Americans and began chatting to our lady from Alabama. Jessica and Leith followed with the camera. Then Rosa thought it a good idea for all of us to sign a menu and present it to the Americans. I was aghast when she went to our lady from Alabama with the menu rolled into a scroll and made a polite little speech.

All the Americans hung on every word she said and when the lady from Alabama opened up the scroll and saw the signatures of a bunch of boozed-up Australians, it was as though she had received a scroll signed by the Queen. She held it up high and showed it to the others who all clapped enthusiastically and gasped in admiration at our scrawled signatures and said what wonderful and kind people we were. I was mortified. But highly amused.

10

Avignon

After our return from Le Paradou yesterday afternoon, the weather threatened again and the skies turned dark. I cursed, I swore, I prayed. If the Mistral returned it would spoil everything. Our guests had not been given nearly enough free time to relax around the pool and they all looked forward to it.

Hester generously invited everyone next door to Ab Fab for drinks and I took the chance for a quiet hour on the mattress in the bunk room. I had not picked up a book or magazine since I'd arrived, I had not been recording my journal nearly enough and I still felt disorganised and out of control.

I wondered if we had been too ambitious with our program. Yesterday would have been easier without the epic lunch at Le Paradou, even though it had been tremendous fun and quite an interesting experience with the Americans. I dozed on the floor and listened to the church bells chime, pondering these and many more issues until after what seemed a very short time the guests returned. I hauled myself up off the mattress and gathered them into the kitchen to watch Françoise, with the help of Maurice, make her renowned *coq au vin*.

Maurice is a lively match for Françoise's energy, and their clashes, while fiery and entertaining, are those of a couple who feel good and safe with each other. They know they can fire up the anger, let it loose for a moment, and then extinguish it in an instant. There is no animosity or malice in their lively clashes, just glorious French attitude. I love it. I just wish I could understand a word they say.

Françoise had asked the farmer to remove the heads from the roosters and to chop up the carcases. She now removed their little round white balls of manhood before browning the chopped portions in olive oil while Maurice stood behind her explaining her methods.

'Once the rooster has been browned in the saucepan, we add the lardons, the little chunks of bacon,' he said. 'Next we warm some cognac in a separate saucepan and flame it and add it to the rooster.'

This process required the two of them—Maurice with the match, Françoise giving him the match-lighting instructions—before the cognac ignited. Maurice then poured the flaming liquid over the rooster pieces and added several handfuls of baby onions to the pan. With much vibrant discussion as to whether the saucepan should have a lid on or not, they brought the *coq au vin* to a gentle simmer and then added a bottle of red wine.

I have made this dish myself at home using chicken, not rooster; it's simple and cooks itself once you have browned the poultry and added the onions and bacon pieces. It was probably one of the most unattractive dishes I'd ever presented as the red wine turned the chicken purple, but it tasted rich and heady. I served it with a creamy garlic mash and green beans and ate it mostly with my eyes closed. Françoise's version did not look purple, more brown and enticing and she served it with a mini-mountain of buttered pasta.

The threatened rain had not arrived and the weather was quite mild, but everyone seemed to enjoy crowding into the cosy dining area in the kitchen of La Petite Maison. It was very intimate around the table and gave us the chance to talk as a group rather than in fractured couples around a long table.

By now everyone in the group was so comfortable with Amanda and I they treated us as though we were old friends rather than tour leaders. They too had grown fond of Maurice and Françoise and we all dreaded the day, looming soon, when they would leave us to return to Lyon.

We were to visit Avignon today, the famous walled city 30 minutes' drive away. Avignon is most known for its Palais des Papes, the grand building that was the power base of Christianity after Pope Clement V moved his papal court there in the fourteenth century. 'It dates back to when Avignon was the centre of the Christian world,' Amanda said at the briefing last night. 'The popes were moved to Avignon from Rome in 1309. The Palais des Papes was the home of the papacy. Different popes added to the buildings during the

Middle Ages making it the largest Gothic palace in Europe. It's a highlight for any visitor to France. You can tour many of the rooms. After the palace, shopping in Avignon is a highlight. There are many beautiful shops.' This last bit was said to a round of cheers from the women. 'These poor women need to shop,' Amanda continued, looking darkly at me. 'They have not been given an opportunity for some proper shopping yet. They have been made to dash in and out of shops with you behind them rounding them up and hurrying them into the van.'

It was true. While there had been free time, it had not been nearly enough. I had not allowed them more than cursory browsing in any of the shops. Today they were free to do what they liked.

We assembled outside the Palais des Papes looking up to the limestone towers, the fortifications and the famous golden Virgin Mary gleaming in the sunshine on the Romanesque tower. Geoffrey addressed the group. He had been doing a sterling job driving everyone safely; I could see the ladies were all fond of him and had put their complete trust in him. There was much discussion about the time we should all meet again once we had split up and it was a long while before a time was agreed and we could all file into the palace where immediately another ticket-buying scrabble occurred.

I thought briefly of the tour guide we met at Le Paradou yesterday who said looking after 100 loud Americans was easy. I find it difficult with just nine well-mannered Australians. While Geoffrey counted heads, for there were more than our nine guests in the group—Maurice and Françoise had joined us, Jessica and Leith were standing by, and if I remember rightly Hester might have been there too, and I think Luce had turned up once again. Confusion reigned and then one of the authorities spotted Jessica and Leith's camera and said '*non, non, non,* no filming.'

There ensued another of those delightfully dynamic French discussions with the usual amount of arm-waving, raising of voices and fast talking as Amanda said she had already inquired about filming and had been told it was permitted.

Amanda strode off to find someone more important than the ticket seller, Geoffrey joined the long ticket queue, the group split up and looked as though they were about to go their separate ways, Jessica and Leith waited with their camera and tripod, I panicked.

It seemed a very long time before Amanda came back. Geoffrey had bought the tickets and advised everyone to go off on their own while we waited. She finally arrived with a triumphant look on her face, waving a piece of paper. 'There, I got permission,' she said and stuck the paper under the ticket seller's nose, and ignoring his glowering look, we all trooped in.

By then I was finding it impossible to relax. The palace, grand though it was, held no immediate appeal for me. And somewhere in amongst the confusion I had lost Geoffrey. I was bereft without him by my side and I realised how much I had come to rely on his calm and reassuring presence. Amanda and I walked from one grand room to another looking for some of our guests to film. 'Now that I have the permission to film, it would be good if we actually had some of our guests to film,' she said. 'It's no good just filming the palace, that's boring. We need people in it.'

So we spent an hour rushing from vast hall to grand room, taking little notice of our surroundings, stopping only briefly to read information boards. We raced from the Stag Room to the massive Grand Tinel where once the reigning Pope dined on a raised platform; we rush through the Pope's bedchamber with indecent haste and gave stone vaults only cursory glances.

We finally found Joan and Shirley resting in a stone arched window looking out to a large green lawned courtyard and ordered them to pose for our cameras. They obliged, as they had always done. In fact, everyone in the group had been so patient and willing with the cameras; they had waited to start their meals while we filmed, agreed to let the camera capture them from any angle, even agreed to being interviewed individually on camera, something I found out later made some of them nervous and others paranoid.

I thought then, as I had so many times before, that God might have sent me a Mistral to deliberately antagonise me, but He also sent me the best group of people in the world to tour with.

After an hour inside the palace Amanda and I ventured outside, me vexing for Geoffrey, she looking forward to lunch. We ran into Ted who strung along with us. We next found Maurice, striding towards us looking Gallic in his striped sweater, in search of Françoise who he had lost in a shoe shop.

'Stay with us, Maurice,' we said. 'We'll have more chance of finding her if we stick together.' Right then we found Geoffrey.

The old quarter of Avignon is easy to explore on foot and it would have been pleasant to stroll for an hour or two, even visit some of its renowned museums, but Amanda knew of an especially good restaurant away from the strip of tourist restaurants outside the palace. She beckoned us forward, past convivial cafés bustling with happy people.

I have always given in to the lure of the tourist restaurant. A bistro or café packed with people eating and drinking has always been an attraction for me yet in so many countries I have experienced disappointing meals in such places. In my experience, the better the restaurant view, the more striking its location, the worse its food. Now Amanda led us down back alleyways and side streets, along an arcade until she came to La Cour du Louvre, where the owners greeted her with three-cheek kisses.

As we pulled up chairs and Amanda flirted with the young waiter, Françoise arrived. We had no idea where any of the others were and indeed, forgot all about them when a scallop terrine, feathery light with layers of mousse, was put before us along with *pichets* of white wine. The *vin du maison*, the house wine, is excellent value in all French cafés so you are obliged to drink a lot of it. The food presentation here suggested a food stylist was at work in the kitchen. Plates of *brochettes*, cubes of thick meat and chicken on skewers, came with thinly sliced green beans and little pots of gratin vegetables. The plate was alive with colour and art, the little pot of vegetables adding a dainty touch and a pretty way to separate the vegetables from the meat.

It was a meal you would save yourself all week for, and at just 25 euros for three courses, a bargain. Although we were full and happy and on to our fifth *pichet* of wine (and Amanda was on the verge of asking the young waiter for a date) we almost fell on dessert: slices of tangy citron and rich chocolate tarts with a scoop of mandarin ice-cream and strawberries.

'Much better than an hour in the Palais des Papes,' I said pushing the empty dessert plate aside before feeling a surge of sacrilegious guilt. I had just been inside a palace where popes once lived and prayed and did important pope things, and yet the highlight of my day had been food.

Amanda laughed at my guilt. 'It's normal, you are in France. Everyone in France puts food before anything else.'

In previous travels to France we had witnessed this preoccupation with food and had read about it in many French travel books. Several years ago on another visit to France, Geoffrey and I stopped at a roadside café on one of the autoroutes (motorways) and found ourselves in an attractive food outlet, the kind of stylish place you would not normally expect to find at the side of a highway.

Outside, giant semi-trailers were lined up in procession; inside, their drivers were indulging in gourmet meals. Although it was a help-yourself eatery, the food in the fridges and on counter tops was of a quality and presentation you might expect to find in a good restaurant. We ate meltingly-good *croque monsieur* sandwiches and fresh salads and watched as the truck drivers tucked into delicate little desserts of crème caramel and pale pink sorbets after they'd lingered over an enormous cheese plate and polished off steaks, *pommes frites* and rich terrines.

Only last year we had stopped at a small town for lunch at an unpretentious café during a tour of the south-west region. A group of workmen, probably from a nearby building site judging by their work shirts and sturdy brown boots, were lunching at a long table. They were eating in the manner we do at home when we have a free Sunday and the whole afternoon to linger over food. They ate pâtés, steaks and roast potatoes with a green salad. They passed olive oil and vinegar to each other and drank several *pichets* of red wine. They finished with a platter of cheese which went up and down the table several times as each man cut off thick slices. This was an ordinary working-day lunch, and it was finished with little cups of strong coffee and a final glass of wine before they all got up and presumably went back to laying bricks and mixing concrete.

Now at La Cour du Louvre we finished our lunch with an espresso and prepared to stroll through the attractive streets of Avignon before meeting our group. Amanda could not resist one last flirt with the young waiter and fluttered her eyelashes at him. I thought women only did that in romance novels, but I witnessed Amanda actually flutter and quiver her mascared lashes at the young man who would have not been out of his 20s.

'Why don't you come to my place on Sunday?' she asked him. 'I am having a jazz concert and a party. There will be 90 people there, you are very welcome to come.'

He said he would think about it and I watched in astonished admiration. How does she do it? Even a woman in her late 30s would think carefully before chatting up a man so young but here she was, confident and friendly, sassy and strong, giving this young man an open invitation to make whoopee with her.

'I'd like to get into his knickers,' she whispered to me as we left the restaurant.

'I think you have a good chance,' I told her, admiringly.

11

French Kissing and Flaming Bananas

*D*espite my anxiety over small matters and not once being dressed and coiffured in the smart manner in which I'd like to present myself, the tour is going extraordinarily well. There has not been a single complaint or even a hint of anything unpleasant between the guests. Usually the role of a tour leader requires a person to also play mother, leader, father, priest, counsellor, confidant, provider and best friend. She also needs to have the kind of diplomacy skills required to bring an end to the crisis in the Middle East, and be prepared to perform CPR as easily as she hands out travel advice. I have not been called upon to give assistance of any kind. No-one has required mouth-to-mouth resuscitation. No-one had come weeping to me over an altercation with another group member. No-one has been an irritant to anyone else. No-one has even asked to borrow anything. These eight guests (nine if we include Gino, which we very much did now) are the most self-contained and self-assured tourists I've ever come across.

Any small stresses I have experienced on this tour have been of my own doing—although I do find it difficult to be patient when all the guests talk to me at once, especially if Ted decides, during a briefing, that it would be the perfect time to tell me a long story about one of his naval experiences. Because he has given his life to me for two weeks and because I am his host, I feel an obligation of politeness and attentiveness to him. So when I am organising all the guests on the upper terrace for pre-dinner drinks, or trying to introduce one of the chefs to them for a cooking demonstration, and Ted sidles up behind me and says: 'Did I tell you about the time in the navy ... I think it was in September 1968 or it could have been October ... ' I cannot ignore him.

If Ted wants to tell me a protracted story, I must pretend fascination. Even Amanda has been guilty of calling my attention to something unrelated when I am in the middle of dealing with the guests. I shall probably never recover from the time I was helping Leith trying to assemble the guests for a tricky piece of filming when Amanda called me into her little office to show me a picture on her computer of *Chocolat's* penis. A fine picture it was too, as was the other one where he stood completely naked by the bed wearing nothing but a strategically placed Champagne bucket.

'Amanda, that's so naughty,' I shrieked when *Chocolat's* penis popped up (pun intended) on the computer screen. I was deeply shocked. 'You're so wicked. What would he think of you showing these pictures to me? It's so outrageous. I can't believe you took a picture of his penis let alone downloaded it on to your computer. You are unbelievable. Show it to me again.'

Gino rarely speaks, just sits quietly by Rosa's side. Every day she appears in a stunning new outfit and as she becomes more glamorous, he seems to become more subdued. What we thought would be a romantic reunion with a happy ending, has turned into an anticlimax, a non-event, and our curiosity to mild interest only.

Luce has returned to Maison de Maîtresse, and she and Maurice and Françoise are having heated discussions at the oven once again. During a particularly lively encounter late this afternoon, something to do with the amount of pepper Françoise should put into another of her savoury cakes, Ted wandered into the kitchen to declare his intention to make an onion tart with the left-over pastry from Dean's *pissaladière* demonstration. Neither woman paid any attention to him. Luce pointed heatedly at the pepper mill and shouted something that sounded alarming, but Françoise ignored her and continued grinding pepper into the mixture until its surface was dotted black. She then cut up large chunks of goat cheese and plopped them into the batter while Ted got in her way with a rolling pin as he searched for the leftover pastry.

Maurice was in the mood to make flaming bananas, a dessert he'd been promising us for many days but had not had the opportunity to make yet—something to do with the weather, he said. He wanted to cook the bananas before our eyes on the barbecue outside, yet each night we had all been cosseted in the kitchen. Tonight we were going to set up the long tables on the upper terrace. Tonight we were going to have an entire restaurant come to us.

When Amanda and I had originally planned this tour, we had scheduled .a visit to La Stalla, a nearby restaurant where the owner, Sebastian, cooked exotic food and provided musical entertainment. But Sebastian had sold his restaurant just weeks before our tour was to take place.

'I will bring the La Stalla experience to you,' he told Amanda when she expressed her distrust of a new owner. And so tonight we would have not only Sebastian and his chefs in our kitchen, we would also have his musicians on our terrace.

We set about moving tables and clearing space on the upper terrace. Then rain threatened. Rain would be a disaster as we needed all the space on the terrace; there was simply no way everyone, plus the band, could fit into the kitchen.

Amanda and I fretted, but our man Geoffrey decided rain, or no rain, we were going to eat outside. He struggled up with the large umbrellas from the lower garden and with much shuffling, knee knocking and loud cursing, he arranged them so they covered the entire long table. He then set about making a dry place for the musicians. By now a light rain was falling and I raced inside for towels to place near steps. Amanda was not pleased that I had her towels on the ground but I insisted we must have some protection.

'I could not live with myself if a guest slipped,' I told Amanda who glared at me and then bustled off to make a bowl of Beaujolais soup.

Finally when we were all ready and the deck was slick, the rain stopped and Sebastian arrived with the food and musicians. A pleasant pandemonium broke out as speakers were hauled into place, microphones were plugged in and wires were wound all around the decks. Amanda made a showy entrance on the terrace wearing a black dress with plunging neckline, carrying the silver punch bowl.

The guests assembled upstairs and anxiously looked to the skies, but their anxiety lasted only as long as it took them to down the first glass of Beaujolais soup and to eat a slice of Françoise's goat cheese cake. Amanda's friend John arrived, a New Zealander living close by and we all automatically called him John New Zealand. He knew St. Maximin as well as Amanda and was to be our market tour guide tomorrow morning. He knew many of the stall holders and had arranged for us to meet several of the cheese providers. He was also going to cook his Provençal sardine specialty for lunch tomorrow.

When speaking English John's accent is pure New Zealand, but when he speaks French he sounds as charming as any French man. He greeted all the women in our group with the typical three-cheeked kiss.

'When did it stop being a two-cheek kiss?' I asked after he had performed several dozen kisses around the table.

'You can do two,' he said. 'But most people here go for three.'

It's very confusing. Geoffrey is especially fond of the three-cheeked kiss and I have seen him perform it in Australia on unsuspecting socialites who have gone in for the one-cheek version. Three-cheek kisses rarely work in Australia. And I have yet to ever get it right despite having delivered and received thousands of social kisses. In fact I am not comfortable with the social kiss at all. It's not that I object to putting my lips onto someone's cheek nor do I mind a set of lips on my own cheeks. It's a question of placing the kiss so it doesn't result in a smashing of lips to ear, nose or eyebrow. Move in too fast when the receiver isn't ready and you could end up planting a smacker right on his (startled) lips. Go in too slow and he will cop you on your (terrified) lips.

And, do we move in for the one-cheek kiss in Australia, or are we obliged to do a two-cheek number? If it is to be a one-cheek kiss, which cheek do we zoom in on first? If it is to be a two-cheek version, which is the correct starting point? You may think this is a frivolous subject, and by God you're right, but when you are horribly inept at the social kiss yet are obliged to perform it at least several dozen times a week, then it becomes an important issue.

In France the social kiss is much easier to perform, and perform it you must. If you meet a friend or even a well-liked acquaintance at the markets in the morning you must greet him or her with an enthusiastic three-cheek kiss, and then after a brief conversation when you take your leave you must perform the kisses all over again. Should you happen to run into the same acquaintance that afternoon in the wine cave, which is a distinct possibility given the French need for continuous wine replenishment, the enthusiastic *bonjour* greeting must be shouted as joyfully as if you had not seen him in years and the zealous kissing must begin all over again. If you bump into him again in the evening while out enjoying a pastis at a local café the kissing must once again be undertaken.

Joanne, our English flower who cooked for us at the beginning of the tour, told me she both enjoyed and disliked the social kiss. 'It's so friendly and nice,' she said. 'It's all right when you have plenty of time but if you run into Amanda at the market with a whole group of her friends, it can take about 20 minutes to perform all the kisses.'

I agree entirely. It is both nice and awful. Once you have mastered an elegant kiss—how to move in smoothly, glide gracefully from one cheek to the other and make a stylish retreat—the French social kiss is a very pleasant greeting; a warm and charming ritual that makes you feel good even if you have permanently chafed lips.

The kitchen in the big house had been taken over by Sebastian and his crew who were busy cooking dozens of plump scallops and threading them on to wooden skewers with juicy prawns. Outside, we sat down to the start of a lengthy meal. The seafood skewers would have been enough but no sooner had we finished them than Sebastian carried out a pot the size of a water tank. It was heavy with a *tagine* of beef, apricots, prunes, coriander and almonds. Sebastian explained the dish at the table and we were once again thrilled with the standard of food. Amanda had come up with yet another excellent chef and one who was prepared to provide this special service just for our group. It was a measure of how much she is loved in the village.

Thankfully the rain stayed away and it turned into yet another magical, luminous evening. The musicians played all the favourites for people in our age group, Gershwin numbers that had us all up dancing and singing.

Gail danced with Ted, and then Françoise and then Shirley. At one point, during an energetic Chattanooga I got her up to dance and after twirling her around several times, tried to pick her up in the air like Patrick Swayze in *Dirty Dancing*. I don't know what I was thinking, but the minute I had her up off the ground, her weight, even though she was very slim, threw me off balance and I fell over backwards. She landed on top of me in a jumble of arms and legs and everyone immediately stopped dancing and looked at us in shock.

There are few sights more unnerving than that of two mature women falling over on the dance floor. I felt ridiculous and stupid, and poor Gail, who had so far been dancing most decorously, must have wondered what had happened. One minute she was twirling and dipping nicely, the next she was on top of me with everyone crowding around her in consternation. Suddenly the ridiculousness of the situation hit me and I went into uncontrollable laughter. Gail managed to get herself up easily but I lay flat out howling with laughter. Maurice tried to assist but my prone weight was too much for one man. He called for assistance from John New Zealand who discovered it was too much for two men. Geoffrey came to the rescue and the three of them heaved and struggled in an ungainly manner until I was up, still laughing, undamaged, apart from my image as a confident tour leader, although I doubt anyone had ever had that impression of me.

The evening continued. Everyone danced. We danced by ourselves, with each other, in a group, in a circle. Françoise and Maurice glided gracefully across the terrace, Luce did a shoulder-shuffle-come-Irish-jig, Jessica abandoned the camera and danced by herself and Amanda showed us how to belly dance. We sang *Just A Gigolo* together and then danced some more. Geoffrey did the twist. I belted out *New York New York* and then attempted my special rendition of *My Way*. The *gendarme* was called.

'It's the cretins!' Amanda cried when she was summoned to the door. Everyone was so caught up in the party atmosphere they barely heard her. This was a group of respectable people, all of them except for Rosa, well over 50. I doubt any one of them had ever been in a situation where the police had been called to quieten them before.

Amanda was back in ten minutes looking agitated. 'I knew it,' she said. 'It was the Number One Cretin. He's a *trou de cul*; he deliberately parked his car outside my front door, turned up his radio as loud as he could to thumping music, left the doors open and ran away and hid. It was him making all the horrible noise, not us.'

I don't know whether it was true, whether it was the cretin and his car radio or whether it was us, but after Amanda had placated the *gendarme*, she settled down.

'What's a *trou du cul*?' I asked her.

'An arsehole,' she replied before laughing and continuing belly dancing. We sang. We laughed. We danced. The night roared on.

Later in the evening I vaguely remember dancing with Amanda, twirling her around until her skirt flared out spectacularly to show her bare bum. I was so shocked by the sight of her round brown buttocks flashing me that I had to lift her skirt to see if she really was knickerless. She was.

Around two in the morning Maurice decided now was the appropriate time to make his flaming bananas. Everyone was bloated with scallops, prawns, meat, prunes, nuts and cous cous, but he had promised us these flaming bananas for five days and flaming bananas we were going to have. He disappeared inside the big house for the brandy and the bananas, coming out to busy himself at the barbecue. With suitable ceremony he brought the bananas to the table, still in their skins, blackened and gnarled and looking like something you would never want to look at in a toilet bowl. With much match-lighting instruction from Françoise, he ignited the warm brandy and poured it over the blackened lumps. Amanda announced she had never seen anything so disgusting in her life and started to laugh uncontrollably until great floods of fat tears coursed down her cheeks. Her laughter was so contagious we all joined in, roaring and snorting and guffawing as only half-sloshed people can at the sight of an ugly burnt banana.

It was one of our best evenings.

12

A Day of Fish and Cheese

We arrived early at the Uzès markets still half asleep and in need of coffee. After making our slow way into one of the little cafés under the stone arcade lining Place aux Herbes we ordered and then lethargically watched a street performer sit on a box preparing his clown costume and elaborate face make-up.

As we were sipping our coffee, John New Zealand arrived, red-eyed and apologetic for his lateness. The kissing began. The women suddenly perked up and keenly joined in as though he was an old and cherished friend they had not seen for a decade, not a stranger they just met last night. Once John had planted 27 kisses on the cheeks of nine women and frightened Geoffrey,

Gino and Ted away, he chatted to the café owner and ordered baguettes and jam for further sustenance with our coffee. John is as well known and liked in Uzès as Amanda, and although he would need to train for decades under her expert tutelage to even come anywhere near mastering her flirting techniques, he is still an excellent flirt, *très coquine* as the French might say. His knowledge of the local area is extensive and his passion for it is clear. As we finished the coffee and good bread and jam, the last traces of our collective hangover disappeared and we took a stroll around the old part of town with John.

Uzès is one of the most graceful old towns in the South of France, and the protected historic section is dominated by the palace of the once powerful Dukes of Uzès. We walked past its massive structure to the church, a lofty old stone building that, according to John, could have a lot more money invested in it to ensure its grandeur is maintained.

'This is all the original work,' he said as he stopped outside the stately church and we all looked up to the high stone walls where dark mould stained the exterior and untidy scrub grew out of some of the higher stones.

'It costs a lot of money to pull those weeds out of the top; it's a constant job. See, there is even a small tree growing up there, birds have nested in it. The church bell still works, it cranks up at seven in the morning and tolls all day on the hour. Where we are standing now is all protected. If you want to do anything to it you have to have special permission. In France it is either no regulations at all, or so many regulations you don't want to deal with it. When it comes to building a new house you never see anybody in authority, but to do something with historical monuments, endless dossiers and papers are required. But it is good because they are really looking after the *patrimoine,* the heritage. The European Union can, and does, have a positive impact. It gives money for historic sites.'

We continued walking around the narrow cobbled streets with intriguing arches and wooden doorways below elegant balustraded balconies and shuttered windows. 'Look at those arches,' John said, pointing to elaborate stone entries. 'They were probably used to park donkeys. All the facades on these buildings tell a story if you dig to find it out. Uzès has spirit. When the summer crowds aren't here I see it very differently. You have the time to build rapport with the locals. I have a friend whose family dates back 800 years in Uzès. There are many people like that here. The past is preserved, tradition is observed. There are *fêtes* and *spectacles* and holidays throughout the year which present an opportunity to remember the tradition and history. There is a reluctance to change. There is a special twist that makes life good here.'

We walked back through a large stone arch along a short alleyway and came into the covered arcades again looking out to the Place aux Herbes where the market was now in full Saturday morning clamour. Jessica and Leith followed us with the cameras.

Determined locals scurried from stall to stall jostling for front place to buy peaches, apricots, tomatoes, cheese, fish, bread and terrines. Children plucked fat red strawberries and glossy cherries from enormous displays in wooden pallets. The enticing stalls held everything from gourmet products to colourful fresh produce and attractive art, craft and jewellery. John stopped first at one of his favourite cheese stalls where he introduced us to Jean-Pierre, a tall thin man with a greying beard. They greeted each other with obvious pleasure.

'Jean-Pierre sells organic goat cheeses,' John said, pointing to the display of cheese rounds. Lined in neat formation in square containers, some of the cheeses were covered in grey ash wash, others had a creamy yellow crust, yet others were pure white. Jean-Pierre cut little tastes.

'These are younger cheeses,' Jean-Pierre said in good English handing everyone a sliver on the end of his knife. 'They are delicious to eat with an aperitif.'

Goat cheese has been embraced by discerning foodies in Australia, but not many others. It is the earthy, almost ammoniac flavour that often startles the palate and takes some getting used to ... and that it comes from goats instead of cows. Although goat cheese and goat curd appear on menus in modern restaurants all over Australia, they still are not eaten in the home in the way the French enjoy them. Indeed, the concerned expressions on some of our guests' faces as they cautiously put the little slivers to their mouths and noses said we had a long way to go to developing a passion for goat cheese.

But not John. 'I eat these young cheeses with a splash of olive oil or a drizzle of honey,' he said. 'They are also great with nothing but a sprinkle of cracked pepper when they are fresh like that.

'All of Jean-Pierre's 100 goats are free range. They have 200 hectares to roam in. They are let out in the morning and they eat all day and come back and get milked in the evening. It takes one litre of milk to make one of these little cheese rounds.

'Jean-Pierre has been making goat cheese for 25 years and selling it at Uzès market. He is one of the market's greatest advocates and he's been instrumental in protecting the rustic integrity of the markets.

'The European Union brought in a rule that all goats had to be tagged. They produced these ridiculously big tags for the goats' ears and because Jean-Pierre's goats are free range, the tags got caught up in shrubs and bushes and it became dangerous for the goats. So he refused to tag them. The idea of the tagging is to have traceability. All European products now have to be traceable by law. Because Jean-Pierre wouldn't put the tags on his goats he wasn't allowed to sell his cheeses at the markets. He got around it though, by giving away the cheese and selling his preserves and other products for double the price. People were happy to go along with that arrangement. He's been very good for the Uzès market. At the same time the EU wanted to stop the sale of olives from open containers here at the markets. They wanted all olives sold under plastic covers. Imagine a provincial market where the olives cannot be sold from big baskets? Unthinkable. The European Union would rather everything was the same for health and safety. Some of their stuff is ridiculous bureaucracy. The EU has a lot to answer for. *Vive la résistance!*'

We moved on past stalls selling delectable terrines and pâtés and *saucisson* to another cheese stall manned by the most jovial man I've ever encountered. He stood behind his glass cabinet with half a wheel of pale cheese in one hand and a large knife in the other, shouting joyfully at us. He cut thick cheese slices and handed them to us. John tried to interpret the man's patter.

'He says he loves the blonde and the brunette,' John attempted and pointed to Sharon and Margaret. He said he would leave his much-loved goats and travel the world with you.'

As gallant as his proposition was, it caused only ribald shrieks from Sharon and Margaret.

'If you go to the sea or the mountain and take this cheese with you it is all you will need,' John attempted to translate again as the man brandished the big chunk of cheese at us. 'If you eat his cheese you will never need to visit the doctor again,' John continued. 'You will have strong legs.'

When the man calmed down for a moment to serve a customer John offered us some background information.

'He has been making cheese for 50 years, since he was 14,' he said. 'He comes from three generations of cheese makers. He is a bit of a character in Uzès.'

A small understatement. The man had finished serving and began to serenade our ladies, the lyrics unknown to us, but according to John something along the lines of him being the best cheese-maker in the country. 'With a good product you will never have any economic decline,' John translated before the man broke into a series of shrill whistles and loud yelps. 'Now he says he doesn't need a dog as he has a dog in his head.' With that little show we thought it time to take our leave.

'Long live cheese,' he called after us as we departed. 'Long live Australia.'

John told us to split up, to go and enjoy all that the markets had to offer. 'Follow your nose,' he said. 'Get out there, ask to taste, you don't have to say anything, it's a body language thing. Just put your hand out. Most of the time they will offer you tastes any way; they're looking to sell, to get people involved in their produce. We will meet at the Café de l'Esplanade at eleven for oysters and wine. If you can't find it, ask a policeman, he's not doing anything.'

Geoffrey and I followed John around the markets, helping him make the lunch purchases: bunches of crisp endive, thick cucumbers, large ears of yellow corn. At the fish stall packed with prawns, mussels, salmon and myriad varieties of fish John bought the sardines.

'These have probably been brought into Marseilles and transported up to the market,' he said. 'In New Zealand we would use these for bait but here they taste good.' He held them up, 'Look at the colour, a little bit of rainbow texture, the eyes are clear, there's a little bleeding around the gills; they're good, they'll be nice at lunch.' Our final purchase was a bag of locally grown tomatoes at two euros a kilo. John sniffed the tomatoes appreciatively as the stall holder handed him the bag. 'The intense flavour,' he sighed. 'This is why we live in France.'

We met at Café de l'Esplanade where Hester and Luce waited for us with their market finds—bunches of fresh flowers and a rakish curly-headed man. Introductions were made, Luce had picked the man up at the market and she looked mighty smitten. I considered telling her to keep him away from Amanda but at around 50, he was far too old for her. He sat between Luce and Hester and seemed completely at ease having a crowd of women descend on him. While the ladies gathered, Geoffrey, Gino and Ted walked around the café looking for spare chairs and I frantically tried to secure a number of tables. The café was packed with Saturday-morning shoppers all enjoying a little respite from the market and as each table was vacated I leapt upon it, picked it up and joined it on to the single one we already had. Within ten minutes I had enough tables for everyone.

Geoffrey continued to round up chairs. No-one in the café seemed to mind me pouncing on them and getting into their space, and again I wondered where the reputation for French rudeness had come from. It must be true as I've read about it in so many books and everyone knows everything you read in a book is factual and correct, then maybe the French have mellowed now that they have to put up with so many invaders in their country. Or maybe it is just my Amazonian appearance. Perhaps they are scared into politeness by me. I am very tall as well as voluptuous.

Amanda and Geoffrey went to the oyster stall and waited while a young man shucked five dozen enormous oysters and presented them on white plates with lemon wedges. Amanda gave us all oyster-eating instructions. 'Take your little knife and cut the muscle which is where it is joined to the shell,' she said. 'Turn the whole oyster over, see how it plumps up nicely because it's had the juice underneath. Then you squeeze the lemon over it and you're ready.'

When she had freed the oyster from the muscle and doused it with the lemon juice, she offered it to me, and the memory of its citrusy, salty taste sliding down my throat is still with me now.

'Have a little sip of your wine to wash the oysters down,' Amanda told us and we needed no more instruction. Within minutes the five dozen oysters had disappeared.

The mid-morning sunshine was now strong and jackets and sweaters were being removed, sunglasses reached for. It was just as glorious sitting there amongst the tumult of the market crowd, looking out to the leafy old plane trees as it had been the first time I met Amanda a year ago.

'More oysters?' I asked the length of the table and to the chorus of 'yes!' I scurried back to the stall to ask the man to shuck another five dozen.

Back at Maison de Maîtresse John set up for his cooking demonstration on the terrace outside the small house, setting out fresh cucumbers, corn cobs, lettuce, fennel, tomatoes, sardines and a bowl of wild rice. In the shade of the leafy old tree he gave us a cooking demonstration so professional and entertaining, Jamie Oliver would have been envious. Glasses of pink wine to hand, the guests listened while he carefully explained how to gut a sardine. The idea of our cooking demonstrations was to not only enlighten our guests about Provençal produce but to introduce them to new taste experiences. But as I watched their frowns I knew with absolute certainty not one of them would return to Australia and ever gut a sardine.

However, John was a pleasure to watch. He made a neat incision in each tiny fish and removed the black, wiggly string of gut in one deft movement. He marinated the sardines in olive oil and salt and then prepared the salad, first standing each ear of corn on its end on a board and slicing downwards with the sharp knife so the little golden kernels tumbled on to the board where he gathered them up and tossed them, raw and fresh, into the salad bowl. He peeled the white layers of fennel from the fat bulb and assembled them carefully on top of each other before slicing through the bundle creating neat white slivers which he added to the bowl. Then after plucking the little green vine tufts off the tomatoes he cut them into neat wedges, using a sharp bone-handled knife he said had once been his grandmother's.

A splash of good olive oil, some red wine vinegar, a grind of pepper and a sprinkle of salt and the salad was ready. Rosa volunteered to cook the wild rice and went inside to the kitchen while the rest of the guests took their wine down to the walled garden to watch John grill the sardines on the barbecue. It was now late in the afternoon and quite some time since the oysters; the smell of chargrilled fish filled the garden.

Ciara had not appeared today, but Hester and Luce were joining us and helped set the long table under the pergola. Plates, cutlery, wine glasses and serviettes soon filled the table and when John presented his sardines there was an appreciative round of applause. What was to be a simple lunch turned into a long and splendid celebration once again. It was almost five in the afternoon by the time we finished with a plate of cheeses purchased at the markets.

'Time for siesta,' I told the group as we collected plates, scraped leftover salad into a bowl for the village chickens and gathered the sardine bones for the village cat.

Everyone was drowsy and still replete with food when we gathered again at 8.30 in the evening for dinner at the local café, Table de Julien. In hindsight, we had planned this badly. To enjoy such a big lunch after a morning at the market and a cooking demonstration, we should have stayed home this evening with nothing but baguettes and water before bedtime. We had been overly ambitious in trying to give our guests so many French experiences and had booked the café with owners Julien and Jennifer who had agreed not to take any other customers this night and to prepare a special menu just for us. The tiny café is just a few footsteps away from Amanda's property and is the only café in the village. Julien cooks, Jennifer works front of house. We ate downstairs in a romantic stone cave-like space. Small candles flickered on every surface, the tables were set with white cloths, good cutlery and sparkling glassware. The atmosphere held so much promise, everyone immediately forgot their bloated bellies and began looking forward to yet more food and wine.

We began with a goat cheese salad and after our experience with the goat men at the market everyone had new respect for this product. Butter lettuce dressed with the vinaigrette we had all come to love complemented a slice of toasted bread topped with a yellow dab of melted goat cheese. It was such a simple dish, yet it opened up the taste buds and had us all looking forward to the next course of fish covered with poppy seeds on a mash with basil and tomato sauce. The presentation was elaborate.

Jennifer, young, attractive and with the kind of dress sense you would expect to see in Paris, shyly explained each dish in her charmingly accented English. The cave buzzed with talk and laughter once again. Dessert was a symphony: a rich crème brûlée served in a small pastry tart and topped with sweet strawberries and a fragile sculpture of golden spun toffee. We waddled out of the café after midnight, marvelling that such a tiny place in so small a village could produce such exceptional food.

13

The Jazz Afternoon and Nipple Tassels

*A*manda has planned a New Orleans jazz concert to be held in her gardens today. She has sold 90 tickets, she has organised Joanne to do the catering, she has sent Geoffrey down to the wine cave to buy 80 litres of wine. Apart from that, she has made no other arrangements. She is a hostess without fear. Not for her weeks of lead-in time worrying over table and seat placement, or whether there will be enough glasses or knives and forks. Not for her stressing over guest lists, budgets or infrastructure.

This morning she burst out of her cave into the sunshine wearing a black-and-white sarong tied halfway up her bosom with a long string of green beads and red metallic chillies dangling around her neck. She immediately began delegating to whoever happened to be out there. Fortunately it was Geoffrey and Ted, both men who like a job. Geoffrey began sweeping and moving tables, erecting a large tarpaulin shade; Ted was told to bring out boxes of glass jugs and bottles from the garage. Joan and Sharon appeared and were sent out around the village in search of wild flowers to decorate the front entry hall. Earlier, Geoffrey had taken some of the guests to Uzès to explore the tempting fashion shops in the small back streets they hadn't had time to give their attention to yesterday.

Amanda's friend Sasha from the next village arrived with her husband Yaan and then work began in earnest. Sasha, whose mother owns a New Orleans jazz club, had suggested the concert idea to Amanda so she felt a certain degree of responsibility for the day. I've never seen party preparation happen so fast. We had only a few hours before 90 punters would arrive expecting a long lunch and a lively concert, but Amanda was as calm as though a family member was dropping in for a quick coffee.

'I'll have the place looking like a jazz club in no time,' she said and then went into bustle overload, picking up a broom, moving tables, encouraging Ted.

Sasha had brought a large box of New Orleans accessories to decorate the tables and garden, and within minutes, colourful black-fringed umbrellas hung festively from trees, strings of colourful beads dangled from pots, feathered and sequined masks lay decoratively on tables. The garden was instantly transformed into a New Orleans street at Mardi Gras.

'In New Orleans you wear masks and dance with these little umbrellas,' Sasha said twirling a bright-yellow parasol, and lassoing a tree branch with a string of red beads before rushing off to embark on another chore.

'Just dust off those water jugs and wine *pichets*,' Amanda called to Ted in the background as he pulled jugs and bottles out of large boxes. They were damp and a little smelly. 'We'll have to wash them,' I said to Ted and we set up a large plastic container of soapy water on a bare table just outside the garage and began the task. Sasha's husband Yaan raced purposefully all over the garden. Geoffrey staggered by with the heavy umbrellas trying to position one over each table. Now the June weather was performing as it was supposed to, and the day was shaping into a hot one.

Sasha was a worker. Petite, pretty and very English, she ran daintily around the garden in her high heels, washing down benches, rearranging decorations, setting tables. It was pandemonium, but we could see results.

'We do this every time I have a big party and there is always total chaos but by the time the people arrive it will be good,' Amanda said confidently, stopping for a moment to lean on her broom before barking at someone into her mobile phone: 'No, no, we need at least 25 baguettes, not 14. There are 90 people coming. Bring 25 at least.'

It was Mother's Day in France and family obligations had called Maurice and Françoise away. They had been with us all week, pillars of strength, towers of comfort, and I missed them dreadfully. They were to return to us late this afternoon to say their official goodbye before going back to their lives in Lyon.

Amanda's daughter, Sam, arrived, with her partner and four-year-old daughter. Seven months pregnant with a lovely big baby bump, she tried to get Amanda's attention for five minutes but it was impossible. Amanda was in party preparation mode and nothing was going to distract her, not even her beloved daughter. I was intrigued by Sam. She appeared so different to her mother: conservative, quiet, understated. Amanda had told me Sam was often shocked by her mother's promiscuity, although she never judged. Sam's own daughter was a mini replica of her and skipped around the garden helping Sasha with the masks and beads.

Joanne had arrived with the food but everyone had been so busy in the garden, no-one heard her calls for help at the front of Maison de Maîtresse. She had struggled by herself into the small house kitchen with large crates and big boxes. By the time I found her in the kitchen she was frantically trying to unload olives, fruit kebabs, *charcuterie* and salads. The men had taken the big kitchen table downstairs for use in the garden and she had nowhere to put anything but on the floor.

I tried to help her plate up the salads and pour olives into bowls but I was very ineffectual working without bench space or table. It was now just an hour before the guests were due to arrive and none of us were showered or dressed, but at least the garden looked festive and ready. The band members had still to arrive. I left Joanne in the kitchen, stepping over bowls of olives, plates of fruit kebabs and platters of cold meats, and went back to the garden to look for Amanda.

'Where is the band?' I asked anxiously.

'Oh, they'll be here,' she replied nonchalantly and ran off into her bathroom to change.

Our guests arrived back from the Uzès shops laden down with bags. Sharon had bought a stunning garment: an oblong piece of fabric that could have been anything. When she pulled it out of the bag to show us we all gasped at its daring. Red and black, it had a definite Spanish look, yet it was pure French chic. It could be wrapped around the shoulders to create a fabulous wrap look or it could be manipulated to form a jacket. It was so French, so absolutely gorgeous I coveted it.

'It was only 100 euros and I may never wear it at home,' Sharon said. 'But I loved it. I couldn't resist it.'

We all tried it on. I thought it looked best on me.

After I'd showered and changed, I went back to the garden to find John New Zealand had arrived, and, surprise and joy, so had Ciara. After pouring herself a glass of Champagne she set up a small table by the door to check in each guest. It was impossible not to like her. She radiated Irish charm. I left her at the door with her

Champagne and then went to look for Amanda again. She was in her tiny bathroom, her hair in rollers, brushing blue eye shadow across her eyelids. Her daughter, who had finally managed to catch Amanda's attention, sat on the closed toilet in the tiny space. I hung on the door, talking to them.

'Sam has been trying to get me alone for five minutes,' Amanda said, putting on thick layers of mascara. 'This is the only time she's had, and look, she has to sit on the toilet to tell me her important news. She's getting married.' They talked of wedding plans, a New Zealand wedding after Christmas. They wondered who might come from France, who would not. I felt as though I was intruding on their short time together, and for want of something useful to do, I washed the dishes cluttering Amanda's narrow kitchen benches. Amanda had received an exquisite silver ring for Mother's Day handmade by Sam. It was a lovely gift from a loving daughter and I felt guilty that I hadn't been able to take on more responsibility so Amanda could spend time with her daughter.

Geoffrey came in and said the band members had arrived: old guys, cool cats, wearing Hawaiian shirts, Panama hats and bandanas; they were outside demanding attention and alcohol while they set up their drums, microphones, instruments and speakers. I went to see if I could help them.

The guests flooded in: French, English, New Zealanders … they came in pairs, in groups, by themselves, in large and small numbers. Cries of *bonjour* mingled with the sound of lips smacking on cheeks. Everyone wanted to sit with their own friends and a great confusion arose. I tried hopelessly to please everybody, racing from the upper terrace down to the walled garden, promising to bring more chairs and rearrange seating plans, with no idea of how to actually go about such chores. Geoffrey caught me mid rush. 'Leave it alone,' he said quietly but forcefully. 'Go and look after your own group, let Amanda worry about these other guests.' He was right, so I never returned to people I had promised more chairs to and went to round up my much-appreciated and familiar group and sat them down at our own table on the small terrace, poured them wine and we all sat back quietly to watch the arrival commotion.

Amanda and I both wore black dresses, hers a strapless daring number which she wore with a black choker at her throat and the green and red chilli beads dangling down her bosom. My black dress was a halter neck, a dress I had bought in Australia that could be worn 21 ways. I remember being giddy with excitement the day I bought it. It is cleverly cut and designed so it can be reconfigured to wear strapless, halter style, Grecian off the shoulder style or plunging-to-the-waist daring style. It's the mother of all little black dresses. With our voluptuous curves filling out the black outfits and our blonde hair freshly washed and styled, Amanda and I could have been twin sisters.

Everyone in our group had dressed up, Margaret showing off her curves in a dazzling orange dress; Sharon poured into a sassy shoestring-strap leopard-print dress. Joan looked elegant in black with the contrast of a pretty red glass necklace she had bought in Roussillon; Eve looked glamorous in a red wrap dress, and Ted looked debonair in a blue shirt and long pants. It was the first time we had seen him without shorts. Rosa looked beautiful in the designer outfit she had bought in Roussillon and Gail flowed in black with an extravagant necklace of dozens of small glittering discs. It was a magical afternoon: hours of rousing music, good food, flowing wine, and such strong friendship between our group I had to keep reminding myself we had all known each other for only a week.

We ate, we drank, we sang, we danced. We put on the New Orleans masks and instantly transformed ourselves into vamps and acted accordingly.

We strolled, wine glasses in hand, from the upper terrace to the lower garden and mingled with the other guests, danced with them, laughed with them, made flippant promises to keep in touch. The rakish man Luce had picked up at the market yesterday turned up; Luce appeared flustered and sat him at her table where he immediately made a pass at Hester. The young man Amanda had chatted up in the Avignon restaurant did not show up but Amanda didn't even notice. The band members drank copiously, broke a dozen glasses and performed energetically. Ciara drank a bottle of Champagne and during a half-hearted debris removal expedition from the garden to the kitchen, stopped and decided now was the perfect time for a dance. 'The Girl From Ipanema' was playing and she rocked to the music in front of the band with a big black bag of rubbish in her arms.

Guests ate every scrap of Joanne's coleslaw, creamy potato salad and chicken brochettes. The baguettes arrived and were cut into neat chunks on an antique guillotine-like instrument, an implement used more than 100 years ago and which is still practical today. The wine flowed. Ciara dropped a tray of glasses. Ted swept up the mess. A large dog appeared from somewhere. A man picked up its front paws and danced with it. Ciara went on to the red wine and danced solo with her eyes closed and an expression on her face that one might have if one had just been given permission to enter heaven. Sharon and Margaret slid their lips lasciviously up and down fruit kebabs and everyone laughed. An Englishman in a safari suit and a pith helmet demanded Jessica and Leith film him. Geoffrey decanted wine from large barrels into small jugs and ran them to the tables like an Olympic sprinter. Maurice and Françoise returned to a rock-star welcome from our group and when we had all finished hugging them, the band members invited Maurice to play his accordion with them. Geoffrey was sent out to the local wine cave for more wine. I knew 80 litres—and that's 107 bottles if you're into conversion—would not be enough.

Maurice played 'Under the Bridges of Paris'. Geoffrey returned and decanted more wine and then he and I danced to 'Ain't Misbehaving'. The rakish man hit on Hester who refused his advances. Then he danced with Sharon. Luce danced with Françoise. A man in red shorts and white shirt danced by himself, a kind of bicycle-riding movement across the garden and back again. The man in the safari suit danced with Jessica. Gino danced with Rosa. Ted got down to some cool moves. The band said they were finishing and we all yelled for more so they played 'La Vie en

Rose' and we all got sentimental and swayed around the garden. Then Amanda made a grand strut down the stairs to say thank you to the band, but instead made sexy breathing noises into the microphone. The rakish man put his arms around Hester who looked uncomfortable. Amanda stopped the sexy breathing and spoke French into the microphone. Then we all sang 'When The Saints Come Marching In.'

Much later, when dusk fell and the last of the concert guests had left, we sat alone, just our gang, with Maurice and Françoise and Luce. We flopped down at the table on the upper terrace and sat quietly talking about the afternoon. Although we had loved the crowd today and met so many interesting locals, it felt good to be just us again. We had leftover tagine in the fridge, so somebody heated it and we lit candles and cut more baguettes and had an impromptu feast. While we ate, Ciara tottered out to the terrace with gifts for everyone.

'It's Mother's Day in France and I want you all to have something,' she said in her charming accent and everyone became overwhelmed. After ensuring Jessica and Leith were filming her generous gesture, she handed each woman a little brown bag of lavender. They all kissed her. Amanda received a separate gift, a package marked 'sexy toys.'

'There's a mistake, that couldn't be for me,' Amanda laughed as she rattled the package and everyone roared.

'Does it buzz?' she continued as she opened it to find a box of candy nipple tassels.

'I'll take them to Morocco and wear them for *Chocolat*,' she said and we all laughed some more and told Ciara how much we loved her, even though we really didn't. Ted asked Amanda to give us a nipple-tassel demonstration. 'I want one to go clockwise and one to go anticlockwise,' he joked and we laughed some more. The evening trundled on nicely, quietly.

Maurice and Françoise said they had to finally leave us and return to Lyon. Maurice made a speech.

'Years ago I took some students on a tour to England,' he said. 'They were never on time. But you Australians were always there. I like this, it is very precise.'

He then thanked each guest and Geoffrey who he called the butler. 'I liked working with you,' he told Geoffrey. He thanked Françoise and kissed her on the cheek. 'She makes the best rabbit, the best soufflé, the best *coq au vin*,' he said and smacked his lips to his fingers. He thanked Amanda. 'I have known Amanda for 40 years. She is very generous at heart. If she asked me for a hand any time, I am always here.'

He didn't thank me. But then I hadn't done anything.

He finally took his leave with Françoise to extravagant kisses and strong hugs. We all had moist eyes.

14

Kayaking, Wine Tasting and Sex Toys

With the departure of Maurice and Françoise so went our morning French lessons. We had intended for the guests to be tutored over breakfast every morning and while this had not happened strictly according to plan—allowances had to be made for the many late starts caused by morning headaches and bleary eyes—we had been given a number of excellent tutorials by Maurice. The guests had written studiously in the diaries we had given them and were now *bonjouring, au revoiring* and *merci beaucouping* with ease. But, unfortunately, they had progressed no further with French grammar and seemed content to keep it that way.

I had managed to give them one travel-writing lesson only, where they had all sat attentively and taken notes. I gave them all a writing assignment and told them it was not mandatory for them to do it, but it would make me happy if they did. I am no teacher like Maurice, but I did manage to give them some good hints on how to make their writing livelier.

'Write me a few a paragraphs about any of our adventures so far,' I had told them without trying to sound bossy. 'If you want, we can go over them individually when you have finished and I can make suggestions to polish them up.'

Only Eve and Ted did their assignments. This morning we sat around the breakfast table while Eve read out a descriptive piece about our visit to the Cathédrale d'Images and a quirky piece about something all travellers would relate to: visiting the toilet in foreign countries. Such is the interest in this toilet subject, entire websites have been devoted to toilet/travel stories and it makes for fascinating, if not squeamish reading.

I was delighted with the two colourful essays Eve had produced after just one lesson. If you recall, she had been travelling for months before she joined us and she had lowered her firm buttocks on to toilets seats of all heights, form and shapes in more than a dozen countries. She had much to say on the subject and had managed to write a very funny article.

Her piece on the visit to the Cathédrale d'Images was so descriptive and captured the goose-bumpy feeling we all experienced so perfectly, I thought (for a guilt-ridden moment only) of plagiarising it. She wrote about the visit to Venice through the images on the cathedral walls, her delight at attending the Venetian opera, her stroll through St Mark's Square and gliding down the Grand Canal. We listened with pleasure as she read aloud. Ted wrote a good piece about his visit to Paris before he met up with us, describing the Parisian streets and buildings in colourful prose.

The others sat quietly and made no mention of any writing attempts of their own. I could not emphasise enough to them, and to you, dear reader, the benefit of keeping a travel journal. It is a quiet pleasure to sit down for half an hour at the end of each day and record your activities and thoughts. It's all about the small detail: the people you met; the food you ate; the mountains, lakes or rivers you gazed upon. The amount of detail you forget is quite astonishing. Street names can be forgotten in a day, restaurant or café names can never be recalled, conversations you had with locals are gone forever unless they are recorded. Even if you never show your journal to another person, it will be a vivid and detailed reminder of a journey you might otherwise forget. And that's all I'm saying on the subject.

Today brings another highlight, if it is possible to experience any more highlights on this joyful tour. We are going to kayak down the nearby River Gardon to the famous Pont du Gard, the 2,000-year-old Roman aqueduct where we will picnic on the banks of the river looking up to the spectacular bridge. One or two of the guests are nervous about this, especially Shirley, who has never embarked on a water sport. I tried to reassure them over breakfast that it would not be a strenuous kayak.

'The river is shallow and calm,' I said to them around the kitchen table.

'No, it's not, it's deep and choppy,' came Geoffrey's voice behind me.

'In parts only,' I added as I saw Shirley's frightened expression.

We were both right. The river was shallow for much of the six kilometres we would kayak, but there were also some deep sections. I did not mention the R word: rapids. I didn't want Shirley to collapse. There was a series of small rapids, hardly anything at all really, although they looked formidable at their approach with the water gushing swiftly over rocks. Geoffrey and I had done this kayak trip last year during our whirlwind trip to Amanda's and found it moderately easy, and we are not athletic types.

Over a last cup of coffee and croissant I tried to reassure everyone of the ease with which they would be able to paddle six kilometres. 'Wear a T-shirt.' 'Yes, have your swimsuit on underneath.' 'Take sunscreen.' 'Yes, you can take Amanda's towels.' 'No, it isn't too strenuous.' 'Yes, the water is smooth.' 'Yes, we will feed you.' 'No, not on the kayaks, on the river bank.' 'Yes, we will all stay together in a flotilla.' 'No, it isn't dangerous.'

It all counted for nothing when we arrived at the starting-point, a five-minute drive from home, where staff at the kayak hire company helped us drag the kayaks to the river's edge after reading out the rules from a poster on the walls. The rules were simple enough:'Wear your life jacket', 'You must have good swimming skills', 'No responsibility taken'—but Shirley spotted one she didn't like at all.

'Look, it says you have to be able to swim under water', she cried in alarm and so I began to calm her all over again.

I told her she could have Geoffrey to share her kayak with. Strong and reliable man that he is, he would personally guarantee her safety and get her in and out of the kayak. In hindsight I think it was the getting in and out of the kayak that bothered her most. Ask any woman over 45 to get in a canoe or on a jetski or up out of a ladder-less swimming pool and she will pale with apprehension. Personally I find it impossible to get back up to a small boat if ever I am foolish enough to jump off one mid-river for a swim. Is it the lack of upper body strength required to pull your weight up as you age? Or the inflexibility of old limbs and joints? In the past, it has taken four strong men to heave me up out of the water and over the side of a small boat and now I never leap into the water without first checking for ladders. Actually, I never leap at all.

When we were all kitted up in lifejackets and had put our gear in the round floating barrels provided for personal belongings on the kayaks, and when the clamour of activity had quietened down— you try getting nine people organised with sunscreen, lifejackets, cameras, towels, kayaks, oars, hats and backpacks, and then getting them all in the river at once for a smooth take off—Geoffrey and I loaded the picnic box on to one of the kayaks and got Shirley safely seated in the front. Jessica and Leith had gone ahead in their kayak with the camera to capture our elegant water entry. At last, after a half an hour of preparation we took off.

Let me stop here and tell you about the Pont du Gard and the Gardon river we are about to kayak down together. This is, after all, a travel book and therefore a book that informs you, not just a frivolous telling of stories about wild parties, multi-course meals and wonderfully promiscuous older women.

Pont as you probably know, is French for bridge. So *Pont du Gard* means 'bridge of the river Gard'. The *pont*, or bridge, is built on three levels, the lower level has six arches, the middle 11 and the upper level 35 arches—it is almost as spectacular a sight as the Roman Coliseum and one that takes the breath away as you kayak around the bend in the river and come upon its mightiness stretching across the river. But this still hasn't explained what it is. It is actually part of a bridge built by the clever Romans more than 2000 years ago to carry water from the springs near Uzès to the Roman city of Nîmes, a distance of about 50 kilometres. It could transport 20,000 cubic metres (5 million gallons for those of you not of the metric persuasion) of water a day. Why the ancient Romans didn't run a pipe along the ground I don't know. Perhaps because plastic had not been a handy product 2,000 years ago, but more probably because the Romans loved building ostentatious structures. It was their gig and they were exceptionally good at it. It is only the top level, a water conduit nearly two metres high and just over a metre wide, that actually carried the water. I think the spectacular lower part was just to make it look awesome. Historians have said it was built around the year 19BC, but newer excavations suggest it might have been constructed in the middle of the first century AD.

I must urge anybody who visits France to make the journey to the south and gaze upon this awesome bridge. You do not have to kayak to it, you can drive there easily and picnic on the banks beneath and then stroll for a short while looking up at it.

Let your imagination wander back to 2,000 years ago and wonder how such a formidable bridge could have been built without electricity, generators, cranes, project managers, tea breaks and hard hats. Some of its stones weigh up to six tons and no mortar was used in the construction. The masonry was lifted by a block and tackle and winch arrangement powered by a human treadmill. Remarkably, or at least I think so, it is believed it took only three years to build with about 1000 workers.

The Pont du Gard is the only section left of the 50 kilometres of the original bridge. From the fourth century it became neglected, obviously other ways to transport water had been invented, and by the ninth century the locals started using its stones to build their holiday homes. It is an unimaginable sacrilege now, but I guess at the time, a big bridge serving no purpose was a handy target for its useful masonry.

Over the years it has been used as a conventional bridge and its outstanding masonry work meant it became a must-see for French masons who journeyed around the country to inspect its work. It was added to UNESCO's list of World Heritage Sites in 1985 and in 2000 it received a 32-million-euro redevelopment. It is one of the top five tourist attractions in France today and we were now paddling smoothly towards it.

We had partnered off: Ted and Gail glided smoothly to the front. Eve, who looked like an Olympic athlete with her flat stomach and girlish legs, went with Joan who kept up the smooth paddling strokes easily. Rosa and Gino made a good kayaking team. I was with Amanda. I dared a look at Shirley, now in the front with Geoffrey and was delighted to see she had lost the terrified expression she'd worn since breakfast.

It was peaceful on the river. We were surrounded by lush green banks and rocky foreshores with clean, clear water all around us. Amanda, annoyed with the restraint of her one-piece swimsuit, had rolled it down to her waist. Free and unharnessed, she paddled us easily down the river and over the rapids with strong strokes, stopping every few minutes so we could dangle our arms in the cool, green water. Within a short time we were more than halfway to the bridge and judging by the smooth speed of our kayakers, no-one was tiring. The river wound its serene way around bends and at times reminded me of the green waterways in Thailand where the limestone cliffs rise majestically from the water. I dared another glance at Shirley and found her laughing excitedly at an approaching rapid, now fully relaxed with Geoffrey behind her powering the kayak easily. Later, Geoffrey told me Shirley said she had been terrified to embark on this water adventure but it was one of the most thrilling days of her life.

We appeared to be the only kayakers on the river today and by the time we turned the bend with the unforgettable spectacle of the bridge in front of us, everyone felt they could have kayaked for another six kilometres. We paddled to a quiet spot on the bank half a kilometre from the bridge and with much ungainly fumbling and unglamorous stumbling, somehow managed to get out of the kayaks.

As we gathered on the bank I felt exhilarated; the river stretched in front and behind us, there was no-one else around. It all belonged to just us. 'How's the serenity?' I shouted down the river, immediately spoiling it.

We laid out our picnic feast on towels on the rocky foreshore: sun-dried tomatoes, creamy brie, moist ham, oily fat artichokes, roasted red capsicum and crusty baguettes. We plucked the ingredients up with our fingers and filled the baguettes while Geoffrey poured wine into plastic glasses.

Rosa took off her bikini top and stretched out on top of a large rock. With the Pont du Gard in the background, she looked like a picture out of a Pirelli calendar. While she sunned her bare breasts, the others went for a swim, gasping loudly as they entered the cool, green water. Geoffrey had bought big blocks of Belgian chocolate and they had melted a little in the sun. When everyone was out of the water, fresh and happy, their skin tingling, he fed us partly melted chocolate and we made little appreciative noises at the pleasure of sticky chocolate smearing our lips.

We cleared up the picnic debris, packed up, scrambled back into our kayaks, to paddle the next kilometre and a half down river to the pick-up point. Gliding under the bridge we saw preparations were being made on a wide area of the bank for a sound and light show.

'They have these *son et lumière* shows in the summer,' Amanda told me. 'They play lights on to the bridge; it's very spectacular.' It would have been yet another highlight for our tour group had I known about it.

It had been another unforgettable day—we had paddled seven kilometres, and now we all felt fulfilled and proud of ourselves. But the day was far from over. On the way back home we stopped at Les Collines du Bourdir, the local wine cave just outside the village of St. Maximin. Although we were all damp from the river and sticky from the picnic food, a wine-tasting had been planned for this afternoon and we were going to do it. Our time was running out, the end of the tour was looming and we still had much to fit in.

We piled into the charming stone building sitting in the middle of green grape vines. 'The wine in here has come from different producers in the region; they bring their wine here and sell it,' Amanda informed.

How Geoffrey had loved each of his many visits to this wine cave where he had mixed with the locals and taken his empty containers to fill from pumps straight from the barrels.

Now we watched in fascination as locals streamed in with various-sized containers and went straight to their favourite wine barrel and began pumping, tapping the sides of their containers when they were almost full to rid them of any air bubbles. We were offered many wines to taste from dozens of the bottles on the surrounding shelves: a viognier, a sweet wine, and a new light red wine, especially made for summer and one that could be chilled.

'Most of these wines do not have those nasty preservatives in them,' Amanda said. 'You do not get horrible headaches with these wines.'

I don't know about horrible headaches but there had been niggling little headaches aplenty on many mornings.

Considering the amount of wine we had bought from this cave, it was understandable why the staff treated us like honored guests. We were offered so many tastes we lost track of what we were drinking; we sipped and sniffed and swirled. We had all been inducted into the pleasures of rosé wine since we had been in France, but now we tasted good reds and fruity whites. When a low-alcohol red wine was offered—'it is just grape juice with a little alcohol'—we all scoffed. 'Too weak,' we said. 'Give us the hard stuff.' I wondered for a moment what I had done to these ladies. Had they all been such good wine-drinkers before they came to me? It was an uneasy thought.

We were back at at the property by six with nothing planned for the evening, so everyone showered and gathered by the pool to gossip. We all had a little story to tell about our observations at the jazz party the day before. Everyone had an opinion on the rakish man Luce had encountered at the market but who had been very taken with Hester. We discussed him for a short while and then talked about clothes and French chic.

Ted did some ironing, and then Amanda turned the conversation to her sex toy collection. How she steered a conversation from clothes to sex I still don't know, but within minutes she had gone inside her cave and brought out one of her buzzing toys. For just a fleeting moment I was shocked. These women might have been relaxed with us, but they were still our guests; they had paid money to be led and protected by us; they trusted us. What would they think? But they all loved Amanda's outrageousness and the toy was passed around, giggled at, and then left to sit on a chair to stare lewdly at us. We sat in the early-evening sunshine until after nine o'clock when Geoffrey came outside, fresh from the shower and dapper in his black shirt and pants, and barbecued spicy sausages for our supper.

15

An Accident in Arles

I have been plagued with fear that some calamity might befall one of our guests—a horrible accident, or, God forbid, even a death. Such occurrences are not all that uncommon on tours and do have a tendency to spoil things. There was that nasty incident at Cradle Mountain in Tasmania not so long ago where four tourists died after their bus rolled off a mountain. Every time we have loaded our guests into the van and fought with the funny foot brake, I have had visions of us rolling down a mountain, not that we have been anywhere near mountains, but you never know. And what if a bridge collapsed while we were crossing it? Every night when I have eased myself clumsily down onto my mattress on the floor in the bunk room and closed my eyes, unwanted fantasies of particular dreadfulness have slunk into my mind. The visions have been vivid, especially the one where we are all in the van tootling happily over the bridge in Avignon singing *Ten Green Bottles*, when suddenly in front of us large cracks appear and instantly turn into massive craters, whereupon half of the bridge breaks away and we hurtle over the edge. So fast does this disaster occur we have only got up to 'nine green bottles' as we plunge into the cold, murky waters of the Rhône.

Then there are the other dreadful fantasies, not so shocking as multiple deaths by drowning, but still disturbing: someone gets food poisoning and has to be taken to hospital and put on a life-saving drip; someone else falls from the top terrace and smashes her face in the geranium pots in the lower garden and loses all her front teeth; and—my worrisome favourite—someone gets mugged on the streets of Uzès and has her organs removed by organ stealers who sell livers to wealthy fat people in America dying of alcohol abuse.

So, each day that we have completed a tour and arrived back whole, safe and with our livers intact, I do a mental little yelp of relief—and then start to worry about what might happen the next day. And now finally something awful has happened (but not to anyone's liver.) (And by the way, we should have been singing *Sur le Pont d'Avignon*, not *Ten Green Bottles* as we plunged over the bridge. I need to refine my nightmarish fantasy.)

Disaster has struck and although it isn't fatal, it's bad enough to cause chaos and anguish for Geoffrey and myself.

Today started out normally with the usual confusion of corralling everyone into the van. It was shaping up to be another memorable day; after our tour of Arles, we were due to meet the mayor of St. Maximin at 4pm. He had heard of our presence in his village and had agreed to put on his mayoral robes and don his ceremonial chains and give our guests an official welcome at the *Marie*, the local council chambers. The *Marie* is where everything official happens in villages throughout France. The *Marie* takes care of all the municipal decisions; you can even get married in the *Marie*. The mayors take their roles most seriously.

We found our way easily to Arles without stress or even a bridge collapsing. After visiting the Arles information centre and arming ourselves with maps, brochures and leaflets, we boarded a little tourist train. These tiny trains look cute and it's tempting to laugh at grownups sitting on a child's train but they are actually very good. They will chug you all over town, chuffing you down narrow roads, around tight corners and along pedestrian areas, while headphones give you a running commentary on all the sights and highlights. They are an excellent way to orientate yourself and I recommend you jump on one even if you feel like a dork sitting on a child's train.

Arles is one of the most graceful and interesting towns in Provence. Established by the Romans during the first century BC, it still has many Roman remains, the most famous is the amphitheatre. At 136 metres long and 109 metres wide and capable of holding 20,000 spectators, it was built as a venue to keep the masses happy while they watched gruesome entertainment. Stage hands could set up trapdoors and other clever devices to enable wild animals to appear from nowhere to rip the heads and legs off helpless victims. Locals loved watching gladiators kill each other, and admit it, we did too when Russell Crowe donned a metal skirt and took to the arena in *Gladiator*. Now the amphitheatre is used for concerts in summer; so much more genteel. It is also a venue for bullfighting, although you'll be relieved to know the bull is not killed. Instead, it comes out with little trinkets dangling from its horns and the toreadors have to remove them without being gored.

The Arles amphitheatre is modelled on the Colosseum and I think it is much more impressive. It never had great chunks removed from it as the Colosseum did a few centuries ago by locals to build houses. Its towering and haughty presence, with 60 stone arches and grand columns, forms the heartbeat of Arles old town. When the little tourist train stops at this highlight there are gasps of awe from every little carriage.

You have to be humbled at the cleverness of the ancient Romans. Not only did they build these huge and solid structures, they did so with such style. The amphitheatre became a fortress in the Middle Ages and defence towers were built which still stand. At this time houses and churches were built in its centre which were demolished in the early 1800s when a restoration campaign began. Now it stands as a remarkable reminder of ancient times, an absolute must-see for any visitor in the South of France.

Arles is also famous for its Vincent Van Gogh connection. The Dutch artist spent a year here during which time he busily painted more than 200 works—and cut off his ear. His favourite café, Le Café la Nuit portrayed in his famous Café at Night painting, is still there in the Place du Forum and is as big a tourist attraction as the amphitheatre.

Amanda had not come with us; she was very upset with Ciara and was going to fire her today. Last night Ciara had turned up for work so drunk she could not focus her eyes and could barely speak or walk. Geoffrey barbecued dozens of fat speckled sausages and Amanda and I made salads. When Ciara finally staggered in as we were about to eat, she made a drunken attempt to set the table in the garden under the pergola. I watched her stagger around the table with a big basket of cutlery, trying to lay down knives and forks. It was actually very funny to so see her squinting with one eye at a knife and looking puzzled at the forks. She finally gave up and attempted to hoist the heavy cutlery basket up on to her shoulder. The weight of it almost toppled her over backwards; I ran to relieve her of it and she went off to do what she always did when she turned up for work, pour herself a glass of wine. At dinner, instead of serving and ferrying wine bottles and bread baskets to the table, she stumbled to a chair and sat down where she attempted to ram sausages and red wine into her mouth at the same time. Geoffrey, who had been busy doing her job, then had to circle the table looking for somewhere to sit until I got up and laid another place. Afterwards, when he and I had cleared the table and washed the dishes, she lurched into the kitchen slurring her intention to clear up. Geoffrey told her to leave. She had to be fired, there was no other choice.

After we had choofed around the town on the train to the main sights including the thermal baths of Constantine, we disembarked and wandered into the centre where we each posed in front of Le Café La Nuit, for photos, annoying the spruiker outside trying to encourage us in.

'Van Gogh cut off his ear here,' one of the group said.

'What, he actually cut it off here in the café?' I inquired and there was much discussion as to where he carried out this gruesome act. No-one really knew, even though they all had an opinion. Van Gogh painted prolifically during his year and a half in Arles but during this time he didn't sell any pictures, was quite poor and suffered terribly from depression. He wanted to found an artists' co-op in Arles and tried the idea out with Gauguin. It was after a quarrel with Gauguin that he was said to have cut off his ear, but actually it was only the ear lobe. Not quite so grisly

We walked in the sunshine, admiring the architecture, stopping at the Place de la République to sit on the edge of a fountain opposite the town hall and dip our hands in the cooling water. These European squares are enchanting, offering visitors a chance to catch their breath while looking at the elegant architecture. Geoffrey and I wandered off with Leith and Jessica to film some of the attractions of Arles. The narrow streets offered doorways and arches leading to private villas and gardened squares, and after a pleasant stroll we paid our money and went inside the amphitheatre, exploring the lower section beneath the arches where they once kept the prisoners and wild animals.

We climbed halfway up inside where Leith set up his tripod and filmed me attempting to be a professional television presenter against the glorious backdrop of the arena. Then we climbed right to the top of the amphitheatre; the ancient stone steps were very steep and uneven but the climb was worth it when we reached the peak. The panoramic views to the Rhône out over the red rooftops and church spires were so thrilling the four of us stood quietly for some long time just staring.

We were by ourselves, having dodged hordes of schoolkids on excursions on the lower levels. When we heard their shrieks and clatter coming up the steps, we decided to leave fast. We raced down the steep stone steps, worn to dangerous and irregular indentations over the past centuries. They were more than a little steep with a very uneven centre.

Then it happened. Leith caught the toe of his large right foot on one of the steps and went flying forwards. I was behind him and watched the dreadful fall, saw the sickening angle at which his right leg went under him. His screams were loud and terrible. There was no question: this was a serious and damaging fall. He lay awkwardly where he fell, white with pain, screaming with agony. We stood helplessly for some moments, trying to comfort him. The woman in the ticket box, alarmed and frightened by the screams, closed her window and shut the big iron gates into the amphitheatre and came running to our assistance. Startled tourists gathered, some handed us their mobile phones. Geoffrey ran to get water. Jessica manoeuvred herself behind Leith in the cold stone stairway and tried to comfort him. I stood by, wretched with impotence. All I could think to do was to fan Leith's face with my map. Sweat had beaded all over his forehead and he was now an awful shade of dirty grey. And still screaming.

'I can't cope, I can't cope,' I said quietly to Geoffrey when he returned with water. 'Yes, you can,' he whispered. 'Get a grip.' I continued fanning Leith's contorted face while the woman from the ticket box talked rapidly at us in French and the crowd around us swelled. More mobile phones were thrust at us.

'I wouldn't even know an emergency number to call,' I shouted at the bearers, rude with distress. By now the schoolkids had all come down the stairs and were leap-frogging over Leith and the scene had turned to awful chaos. Finally the ticket office woman made a telephone call and within minutes sirens sounded outside the amphitheatre. Three men dressed in immaculate blue uniforms with brown leather boots strutted haughtily into the amphitheatre. They were *pompiers*: firemen specially trained to treat emergencies and drive impressive red vans. They took in our awful situation— Leith whimpering now, Jessica pale and upset, me fanning Leith with my map; Geoffrey grim and quiet—and said: '*Parlez vous francais?*'

'No, we are dumb fucks who don't have a word of French which would have been very helpful right now,' I said, but only silently to myself. To them, I indicated we did not speak French and they in turn indicated they did not speak English. Our eyes said it all: it might be helpful if we could understand each other.

Pompiers, to my knowledge, are not actually allowed to administer first aid or give pain relief. Their job is to get the victim to the nearest professional assistance, and so, after some consultation between the three of them and some gentle prodding of Leith's leg, a pair of scissors was produced.

We all looked alarmed for a minute until we realised they were going to cut Leith's trousers. Leith was quiet now but still a horrible grey and in agony. He half sat, half laid in the position he had fallen, terrified to move his leg drawn up underneath him at an impossible right angle. He was not happy about having his trousers cut, but the *pompiers* cut them anyway and after more consultation and discussion they went to their red van and brought out a stretcher, struggled to place it beneath Leith, then pumped it up with a pumping contraption. It was impressive to watch as Leith was lifted gently up on the stretcher which grew quietly beneath him. As they loaded him into the red van with Jessica by his side I felt my heart break. I had no idea where they were going. The *pompiers* tried to explain but the language divide between us was total. Even the woman in the ticket office had no word of English and the tourists, some of whom might have been able to help with translation, had disappeared. Finally, one of the *pompiers* went to the ticket box and got a map. He held it to the wall and drew a line on it, I assumed to the local hospital. He handed it to me and with some fast, but obviously reassuring, French words he went back to the red van.

Geoffrey and I stood miserably outside the amphitheatre watching them drive off. I felt desolate.

Now, I realise this accident is nothing compared to awful injuries and terrible illnesses some mothers have to nurse their offspring through, but I was inconsolable with grief for Jessica and Leith. They had come to France to please us. They had worked 16-hour days filming us without promise of a cent for their efforts. They had rushed about so frantically they had not had time to appreciate any of the highlights we had all enjoyed so much. They were just a few days away from the end of the tour when they would pack away their camera equipment and go to Mykonos, where they could finally relax and have their honeymoon. And now it was all ruined.

Back at Maison de Maîtresse, the guests were suitably sympathetic, but looking for wine and fun in the garden before preparing to go out to dinner tonight. They had become fond of Jessica and Leith but understandably, after some initial condolences to Geoffrey and I, they dismissed any thoughts of drama and disruption.

'I can't go on with the tour,' I wept to Geoffrey in the privacy of our tiny bunk room. 'I can't bear to think of Jessica and Leith in a foreign hospital without communication skills facing God knows what. I have to be with them.'

'We will continue as though this hasn't happened,' Geoffrey said quietly. 'It's our responsibility. Be strong.'

He was right, of course.

And so we went downstairs to join the others in the garden, pretending this unfortunate accident was a mere hiccough. Tonight we were to go to Tractor, a local restaurant of some renown where the chef had prepared a special menu for us. The gang was gathered around the pool, Ted at the ironing board. Amanda was a godsend; she immediately got on the telephone and established which hospital they had been taken to in Arles, when we could speak to a doctor, when we might be informed of the diagnoses and prognosis, how to contact the travel insurance company back in Australia. It was busy and unsettling but I forced smiles in front of the guests and pretended calm. After a dozen calls and some small insight—it was not good, Leith would have to either have an operation now, or be flown home immediately to have surgery in Australia—I found a quiet spot to myself in the garden. I wanted to hold my head in my hands and sob for Jessica and Leith and all that they would have to go through to get home: all the drama of surgery, dealing with an insurance company, getting home with a leg in a cast, the loss of working hours in their business, the financial concerns they would encounter—it was going to be rough. Margaret bounced over and joined me.

'Have you seen my toe ring?' she said brightly. 'I think I lost it in the pool.'

I looked blankly at her happy face. She was a darling, so vivacious and easy-going, and obviously enjoying every moment of this tour, but her toe-ring timing could not have been more inopportune.

'Quite frankly, I don't care if your toe develops gangrene and drops off,' I said, only half joking. 'I'm sorry but I have other more pressing matters on my mind right now. I just cannot turn my mind to searching for a toe ring.'

She laughed good-naturedly and then so did I. I felt better. I apologised to her and said I really did care about the health of her toe, did not wish a flesh-eating disease upon it, and tomorrow I would help look for her toe ring.

The evening was a blur. Tractor must have been an old farm at some stage; it was in the middle of the countryside, along the end of a dark road outside Uzès. I do remember the place being crowded with people. I remember John New Zealand joining us, and Hester coming along with New Zealand guests she had staying at Ab Fab. Her guests had just arrived from Spain where they had been carjacked and mugged and were still traumatised. The woman bore signs of the attack with dark bruises around her neck. They believed their attackers had seen them at a road-stop having coffee, guessed they were tourists with money and valuables, had driven on ahead and laid deadly spikes on the road. After the New Zealanders had run over the spikes and got out of their car to inspect the deflated tyres, the muggers pounced, grabbing the woman around the neck, pushing the man into the car, stealing their bags, money, cameras and other valuables.

That awful scenario was one I had not thought of for our guests. It now presented something fresh for me to worry about.

We ended up being a group of 20 once again at a long table inside the restaurant. Within half an hour of our arrival the noise level had risen dramatically and we became one of those large groups who annoy everyone else in a restaurant. I remember the food being good and plentiful, I remember the ladies' loo being an extravagantly decorated boudoir with a plush red velvet chair in it, I remember sitting in it for a photo in turn with the others, I remember going through copious bottles of wine which shocked Geoffrey who had to pay the bill. I remember everyone having a noisy good time. But all I wanted to do was go home, lie down on my mattress and weep.

16

Mini-skirts, Fishnets and Paella

*I*t wasn't until I woke up this morning, stiff from the mattress but briefly enchanted as always by the sound of the church bells ringing, that I remembered the mayor. I hadn't even given thought to our meeting with him yesterday afternoon after the drama and I suddenly had a vision of him still sitting waiting in his office dressed in all his finery with his chains clanging gently around his neck. I rushed downstairs to find Amanda who assured me she had called him and informed him of our situation. Yesterday had been the only opportunity he could give us for a formal welcome; unfortunately, he would not be donning his robes and chains for us again.

We had a day off today, our first full day to spend at leisure and it couldn't have been better scheduled for me. I wanted to think about nothing other than Jessica and Leith and try to help them, even if it was only to give them Geoffrey. I am so very fortunate to have a calm and reliable husband. In the 40 years we have been married he has always been the one to guide us through any misfortune and thank God, there have been only small troubles throughout those blessed 40 years. It was he who faced up to school principals when summons came from schools; he who helped Jessica through a roiling hormonal time in her teenage years, he who took our son Steven to Puckapunyal when he joined the Army Reserve because I couldn't face saying goodbye; he who went searching for our youngest daughter the night she climbed out of her bedroom window and ran away during a teenage tantrum. Now he was helping me stay focused and controlled to ride through this unfortunate accident.

We telephoned the hospital to be told Leith would go into surgery this afternoon and could be expected to stay in hospital for at least 15 days. Jessica was brave. When we had spoken to her briefly last night at the hospital, we told her to go out and buy some warm clothes, some food and wine.

'How can I bring wine into a hospital emergency ward?' she asked.

'Just take it in, no-one will mind,' we told her, even though we were not sure if this was correct.

'How will I open it?' she said. France has yet to embrace the efficient screw-top we so love in Australia.

'It's France,' we told her. 'Someone will have a corkscrew.'

Jessica said the hospital emergency staff had been wonderful. One of them spoke fluent English and explained procedures to her while Leith had examinations and scans. The staff member even took Jessica out to nearby shops to make her small purchases. But this morning, he was not on duty and she was alone without a translator and feeling frustrated. Amanda and I drove into Arles to pick her up and bring her back. All the way back as she sat squashed into the back seat of Amanda's convertible, I leaned over and stroked her legs and arms and asked her how she was she coping.

'It's all right, I'm all right,' she said.

'But you are going to miss out on your honeymoon in Greece,' I wailed.

'We can always come back another time. It really is okay.'

But it wasn't. Leith had to have a steel plate put in his leg and many pins inserted to hold it. They were going to cut his leg open this afternoon and it would be months before he could walk normally again. All I could do was to help Jessica make arrangements to get Leith back home to Australia, and thank God, their insurance company was co-operative.

There was no quibbling, no hedging, no interrogation, just a helpful woman on the end of a phone in Australia who comforted as well as assisted. We did not know at this stage whether Jessica should go and find a hotel in Arles and stay there to be near Leith, or whether she should stay in St. Maximin. We did not know whether Leith would be allowed back to Australia on a plane with a heavy cast on his leg and I had visions of them being stuck in France for the next six months.

However, I could let none of these fears be known to the guests. They had to think I was in control and that they came first. Back at Maison de Maîtresse while I helped Jessica pack some of Leith's clothes and toiletries and scurried around looking for suitable books and magazines for him, some of the guests wanted to visit a supermarket. Geoffrey drove them into Uzès. French supermarkets are excellent. Their cheese displays are epic—with so many varieties, choosing is almost impossible. Fridges hold sausages, pâtés, *rilettes* and tempting *galantines*. The ready-cooked dishes set you salivating—the *brandades, cassoulets, coq au vins*—all as good as you could make yourself (often better quite frankly).

Everyone came back from the supermarket excited about the choices and made plans to each prepare a special dish for our farewell party on Friday night. They were all due to leave on Saturday morning and we wanted to make this last night special. Amanda's son was coming with his DJ equipment even though she had fears about pushing the cretins to their limits.

In the afternoon Amanda took Jessica back to the hospital to deliver Leith's clothes and toiletries. I waited for Michel's arrival, the last of our chefs to demonstrate.

Michel is a gentle yet mischievous gay French man. He is married to Johnny, an earthy and practical cockney. They operate a *chambre d'hôte* about 40 minutes' drive from St. Maximin where they pamper their guests in a typical French provincial manner.

We visited their lovely property last year during that heady week with Amanda when Michel and Johnny threw a lunch party for 50 guests in their neat gardens. I recall meeting a lot of English people that day, all sea changers who had left the damp of the UK for the sun of Provence, all of them happy to be living in Provence, none of them speaking French, nor intending to.

Now Michel, the cooking half of Johnny and Michel and the one who gives his guests sumptuous meals in their antique-filled dining room, had agreed to come and demonstrate his specialty for our guests, a very un-French *paella*.

'He wants to dress up in his mini-skirt,' Amanda told me earlier. 'He loves to wear it with fishnet stockings, suspenders and stilettos. Do you think the guests will mind?'

Mind? After being subjected to Amanda's naked boobies and barely covered bottom almost daily, having had to wear her lurid boas to keep warm, having accepted an invitation to watch her use her nipple tassels and been given a brief but informative demonstration of one of her sex toys, I told her I did not think Michel and his mini-skirt would pose a problem.

I love Michel. I don't know whether it is his soft voice and seductive accent, his admission to being 'a naughty boy' or his flamboyance with the skirt and stockings, but I adore him. He is as opposite to Johnny as it is possible to be: the gentle Frenchman and the earthy cockney. But they've been together for more than 20 years and committed to each other in a French ceremony called *pax* which binds them by law as in a marriage.

'I love him, din I?' Johnny had said to me a year ago on that first night we met them both in Amanda's garden. He had looked across to Michel, chatting elegantly to Amanda's friends and repeated 'bloody love him, I do.'

Michel loves him back, as Johnny allows Michel a certain amount of freedom, especially to go on little mini-breaks with Amanda. Michel and Amanda make good travelling companions and it was on one such trip in Morocco where Amanda met *Chocolat*. Michel had pointed out the handsome man at the hotel and Amanda quickly moved in.

Now Michel arrived at Maison de Maîtresse around four in the afternoon while Amanda was driving home with Jessica from the hospital. He came with an entourage of just one, not Johnny, he was left at home looking after their own guests. Together Michel and his entourage man hauled in a giant box of ingredients for Michel's culinary specialty. We sat in the kitchen of the big house and drank a glass of red wine and then another. I loved catching up with Michel, listening to his cheeky stories, told in his dreamy accent. We sat for a long time and ended up finishing the bottle by the time Amanda returned and discovered we had no *paella* pan.

'Where's the bloody pan?' she shouted the minute she came in the door. It was the same pan Rosemary had used to cook her

Spanish seafood dish. I don't know where it had come from, who had brought it, but now it was gone and Michel could simply not cook *paella* for 20 or more people without the correct pan.

'I hope Rosemary didn't take it back to Spain,' I suggested stupidly. The pan was the size of a semi-trailer tyre.

'Where is it?' Amanda cried again and there followed 15 minutes of high drama while we hunted for the pan. I thought of suggesting using the big pan Amanda had bought at the flea market but I could see she wanted a genuine *paella* pan. Eventually, the entourage man was sent off in his car to chase up another *paella* pan somewhere in the village and calm settled on the kitchen once again.

'I must get into my mini-skirt and heels,' Michel said after a short while and went off to change. Amanda and I decided it might be fun if we all went a little flamboyant and wore boas; she bustled off to find the ladies and Ted and Gino.

When we had the group out on the upper terrace garlanded with colourful feathers, Michel made his grand entrance wearing a white T-shirt with sparkling silver dashes, a black mini-skirt, fishnet stockings and black high heels. His purple boa was wound twice around his neck and as he strutted out on the terrace all the ladies let out a loud cheer. Ted and Gino watched cautiously.

After countless photos had been taken of him, and after he had turned his back to Jessica with her camera and cheekily lifted up his mini-skirt to reveal a beautiful pair of see-through nylon panties covering two firm and feminine buttocks, we watched him lay out his *paella* ingredients.

He set out big green prawns, white squid, tiny orange shrimp, fat yellow chicken legs, strips of red pepper and onions, little pink *langoustines*, rounds of spicy *chorizo* sausage and a large bowl of shiny black mussels. Geoffrey came out and began pouring wine. The ladies all wanted a turn at hugging Michel, kissing his smooth cheeks, having their photograph taken with him.

Then the *paella* pan arrived with the entourage man and there was another loud cheer.

The evening had begun.

Michel might have been flippant about his dress sense, but he was serious about his cooking. He heated olive oil in the giant pan over the barbecue hot plate until it sizzled and then he carefully placed the chicken pieces in one at a time, filling the enormous pan tightly. We watched the chicken splutter and brown before Michel turned it over with his tongs and sprinkled it with sea salt and pepper.

'I will let this cook for 10 or 15 minutes,' he said and hoisted up his leg to show us all his suspenders before continuing on normally: 'Then I will take it out and keep it aside.'

After another quick flash of his knickers and another glass of wine, he removed the browned chicken pieces and laid them on a plate. Next, the squid went into the chicken-flavoured oil with the strips of red pepper and sliced onions. He stirred the colourful mixture until it was evenly spread over the giant pan and then sprinkled it with a mixture of dried saffron, turmeric and pimento.

'This will give it a lovely colour,' he said, stirring and coating the mixture with the spices. The smell was tantalising and we gathered excitedly around the pan. When everything had sautéed for five minutes Michel showered the pan with rice from a large bag, lightly raining it over the ingredients.

'We don't want to use too much rice; we want to let the seafood be the star,' he said as he poured chicken stock into the pan and then tossed in the tiny pink shrimps.

'Now it is time to return the chicken to the pan.' He carefully laid each chicken piece on top of the mixture to form a circular pattern.

'It is important to make it look pretty,' he laughed. 'I like everything to be pretty.' This announcement called for another flash of his panties; the ladies yelped their approval and called for Geoffrey to bring more wine. Other people arrived: Hester, looking chic in a stylish French dress and little white sweater, a man in a striking pin-striped jacket, and a French couple we had never seen before. I greeted them with the warmth I normally reserve for cherished friends. By now I had learnt that everyone who dropped in to Maison de Maîtresse was interesting and welcome.

Michel sliced the chorizo into neat circles and placed it amongst the chicken, making sure every centimetre of the pan received plenty of sausage, then he added the green prawns, positioning them on top of the rice and stock, in between the chicken pieces. Next he scattered the little pink langoustines over the lot.

'What are langoustines?' one of the ladies asked.

'Like your little lobster,' Michel replied and a langoustine discussion broke out among the guests and continued until Michel made the final touch, gently pushing the shiny mussels into the mixture so they stood, poking up mischievously between the chicken and prawns. By now the *paella* pan was almost overflowing with luscious ingredients and looked as though it could have fed 100 people. After everyone took a turn standing by it for a photograph, Michel covered it with foil and announced: 'We must leave it to cook for 15 minutes. Bring me some more wine.' And with that, he showed us his panties one more time, sat down and crossed his legs prettily.

17

The Sainted Marys and the Gypsies

This morning we telephoned the hospital to learn Leith has had his operation. Twelve pins have been inserted in his leg; he has been cut from the top of his outer thigh almost down to his knee. Other than that we could get no more information. We still had no idea how long before he might get home to Australia or where he and Jessica will stay if they have to stay in France for some months. Geoffrey, Amanda and I were due to leave St. Maximin ourselves on Sunday for Greece. We had booked small villas each in the same beachside resort in Mykonos as Jessica and Leith and now we had reluctantly cancelled Jessica and Leith's villa. I also wanted to cancel ours. I felt quietly distraught about going to Greece without them. Jessica is 30 years old, a married woman with a husband almost 35. They run a successful business in Australia and have built themselves an admirable property portfolio. They are hard-working, capable people, yet they are my children, my responsibility. I was deeply troubled and riddled with guilt at the thought of leaving them alone in a foreign country while I went off to laze on a Greek island. Is it possible to ever stop worrying about your offspring no matter how old you or they grow? I have yet to become a grandmother and after yearning for grandchildren for some years now, I'm not so sure I want all the worry and anxiety that will surely come with the addition of another family member. I concern myself over Jessica now that she is 30, the same way I did when she was three.

Now I would have much preferred to stay in France with her and Leith and forget about Greece, but Geoffrey quietly assured me it would serve no purpose.

Amanda was helpful. 'Jessica and Leith can stay in my apartment if Leith comes out of hospital while we're away,' she said.

'How will he ever get in and out of this property?' I countered. 'That staircase is a terror to get down for an able-bodied person, let alone anyone in a wheelchair.'

We tossed the problem around, Amanda and Geoffrey offering ideas, me rejecting them, Jessica being brave. The insurance company was on the telephone from Australia every few hours. Many suggestions to get them home were put forward, including the hiring of an ambulance to get Leith comfortably from Arles to Paris where he would be assisted on to a plane into first class with a flat bed. Hotel options in Arles were looked at should he be unable to fly home for some time. If there was anything to be learnt from this it is the value of travel insurance. We had no idea how much Leith's operation and hospitalisation would cost, but surely it would have run into the thousands. And a first-class air fair home? Unthinkable. (Although I might consider breaking my own leg if it meant I'd get a seat up front. A flat bed and attentive staff urging expensive Champagne on me could be worth a snapped bone.)

It was all complicated but nothing could be finalised or even arranged until we had spoken to the doctors. Amanda promised to keep in touch with the hospital throughout the day.

I did not let my worries show to the guests. We had another big day planned with two excursions. In the morning we were to visit Saintes-Maries-de-la-Mer and in the afternoon Aigues-Mortes.

We took off early in convoy once more: Geoffrey with the gang in the van, Rosa and Gino in their car, Amanda, Jessica and I in her silver sports car. We dropped Jessica off at the hospital in Arles and as I watched her go inside the big building, smiling bravely and waving back at me, I felt wretched all over again and sat silent and miserable all the way to Saintes-Maries-de-la-Mer.

Saintes-Maries-de-la-Mer is most famous for its gypsy pilgrimage each year to celebrate the legendary arrival by boat in

AD18 of Mary Magdalene, St Martha and the sister of the Virgin Mary. Every May during the pilgrimage the town is alive with music, dancing and festivity, and some say it is one of the most vibrant festivals of the many held all over Europe each year. Saintes-Maries-de-la-Mer means Saint Marys of the Sea. It was once a small fishing village, now it appears to have grown to a seaside resort town for English tourists. The number of newly built hotels and resorts on the outskirts was evidence of the continuous growth along most coastal areas of Europe.

On the Mediterranean coast near the heart of Camargue's national park, Saintes-Maries-de-la-Mer is surrounded by the immense plains of the Camargue. We drove through these plains, flat and fairly uninteresting but for the handsome ranches where beautiful white horses, famous in the area, are bred. If you happen to be a horse person that will excite you. As it was, no-one in our group even mentioned the ranches or horses when we arrived and parked the van and cars in the car park near the port. No-one seemed particularly interested in the gypsy pilgrimage aspect of the town either—perhaps because we could see this was a place very much overrun by tourism. Across the road from the car park dozens of little restaurants and cafés beckoned tourists with specials of English and Spanish food and tourists paraded by in shorts and T-shirts.

Archaeological excavations have shown Saintes-Maries-de-la-Mer to be a holy place, inhabited by a number of cultures including those peripatetic Romans. This is the place where the

Christianisation of France originated. According to legend, Mary Jacobe and Mary Salome who were close relatives of Jesus and Mary, arrived at Saintes-Maries-de-la-Mer when they were expelled from Judaea during the persecution. With other expelled Christians they brought the Christian belief to this region. But there was a third Mary who is now celebrated in the pilgrimage each year. A black Mary. Her origin and identity are shrouded in mystery. Some say she was a powerful local queen who welcomed travellers, but others suggest she might have been an ancient pagan goddess or a black Egyptian slave of Christ's mother Mary. She is the patron saint of the gypsies, quite the enigma and her cult still persists today.

'The gypsies have always participated in the pilgrimage,' Amanda told the group as they assembled by the van. 'They come by the thousands every May. They used to come in horse-drawn carriages painted in bright colours; the colourful carriages inspired Van Gogh. Now the gypsies travel in modern caravans but they still preserve customs and traditions.

'They come from all over Europe and even from other continents. For about ten days they make camp in the streets and squares and on the beach. It turns into a huge festival with music and dancing in the restaurants and on the streets.

'The ninth-century Romanesque church is well worth a visit. The gypsies all visit the church and light candles. It's a very special place.'

The pageantry surrounding the parading of the three Marys is said to be spectacular. The Marys are taken down to the beach by the gypsies, the appointed guardians, and the Camargue cowboys on horseback. The parade goes right into the sea to symbolise the arrival of the women saints at Saintes-Maries-de-la-Mer. The sea is blessed, the land is blessed, everyone in the parade is blessed … and then it is time to head back to shore to party.

No-one in our group seemed particularly interested in gypsies or black Marys or parades of great pageantry. 'Where are the shops?' they asked as we walked into the town. Of course it would be an entirely different matter if we were there in May during the festival. I could imagine the colour and excitement, the stirring sound of the gypsy violins and guitars, the women in their long, colourful skirts and white gypsy blouses, the dashing men wearing kerchiefs tied around their heads with wisps of escaping black curls, small gold hoops in their ears … hey, I'm getting a bit carried away with the gypsy romance here. The reality is, Saintes-Maries-de-la-Mer is just a typical and pleasant seaside town minding its own business on the Mediterranean coast for most of the year. We strolled across the road and began to look at the restaurants and shops.

The group split up into twos or threes and went off, most of them to find shops. Amanda, Geoffrey and I wandered the busy streets. *Paella* was the main event here, and if we hadn't indulged last night in the best *paella* imaginable, we would have been tempted.

We ate at a small café surrounded by tourists. Amanda and Geoffrey indulged in a giant dish of tellines, tiny things in shells, similar to the pippies the New Zealanders so love. Geoffrey is also a New Zealander, although he often forgets this as it has been so long since he left his country, but like Amanda, when he comes near any seafood that reminds him of his childhood digging pippies from the sand on the local beaches, an almost insane craving takes place. I could not be bothered with these little crustaceans; all that opening the tiny shell to pick up a toothpick-sized portion of flesh is just too much hard work. But Amanda and Geoffrey thought this was gustatory paradise and as they prised open the little shells and popped a microscopic morsel of meat in their mouths I ate a niçoise salad and amused myself watching their blissful expressions.

It was a pleasant morning and after a wander along the fetching beachfront and the Port Gardian, we met everyone back at the van and drove to Aigues-Mortes. This is a perfectly preserved walled town, a fortified city built in the thirteenth century to provide an important port on the Mediterranean. The ramparts and circular towers, the walls and gateways, the sense of the past should appeal to anyone interested in learning, but the familiar question from the group, as they prepared to split up and wander on their own, of 'where are the shops?' obviously meant no-one would return with exciting stories of historic discoveries.

Aigues-Mortes was the starting point for the crusades. Vessels gathered here prior to the journey to the Promised Land. The Tour de Constance, a round tower adjoining the ramparts, was used to hold Protestant prisoners in the seventeenth century, the best known of them being Marie Durand, who was taken there at the age of 15, simply because her brother was a Protestant, and held for 38 years.

The walled centre is very touristy now, filled with shops and restaurants. Amanda and I had an hour to ourselves; Geoffrey went off with Gino and Ted for a beer in one of the restaurants in the main square. I had rarely been alone with Amanda and it was lovely to spend some quiet time with her, sitting in a patisserie indulging in a pastry. To my mind, French patisseries are better than French designer shops. Give me a window full of fruit tarts with their jewelled tops of mandarin segments and rounds of green kiwi fruit; let me stare at sweet brioche, delicate friands, chocolate éclairs and creamy custard tarts. It's far better than looking in a window full of Louis Vuitton or Chanel any day.

After we had enjoyed little chocolate mousse cakes, we went in search of clothes. It's not a good idea to try anything on when your stomach is full of chocolate mousse and I can't say I enjoyed our little expedition. However, Amanda did. She is not shy about marching into a dress shop, asking for something in her plus-size and trying it on, often in the centre of the shop if the changing rooms are small. It tends to be quite diverting for people passing by outside, not to mention for the sales assistants, and so we stood in a shop while Amanda disrobed to her bra and panties and tried on a number of white tops. I tried to shield her from the passers-by but it was useless. She decided on a smart white top that looked so good on her I bought one myself without trying it on. If it would fit Amanda, it would fit me.

We reconvened at the van, the ladies laden down with shopping bags, Ted without a purchase, Geoffrey and Gino looking relaxed.

We were to pick Jessica up at the hospital on the way home and to save the guests making a detour it was decided Amanda and I would go alone and for some reason I cannot now recall, Gino came with us. This was the first time we had been alone with him. Amanda, who had been involved in his romantic mission days before our tour had started, could not resist asking him why he had come all this way to be with someone we weren't too sure still wanted him.

He was reluctant to talk at first, but Amanda's gentle questioning slowly brought him around and for the first time in nearly two weeks, he talked. Now I'm not going to reveal here what he told us about his situation, it was deeply personal and nobody's business but his and Rosa's (and now mine and Amanda's.) But I will say, even though Gino was not a happy man that day, he was a persistent one and his determination to keep his marriage going was admirable. He talked all the way to the hospital while we listened sympathetically. By the time we parked the car in the hospital grounds, Gino was a new confident man. He came into the hospital with us and up to Leith's room where we found Leith miserable and frustrated.

'I can't understand anything that is going on,' he complained which is hardly surprising as he doesn't have a word of French.

'The doctors have just come around and looked at my leg and congratulated themselves on what a good job they have done; hospital food is crap, the room is stuffy. I want to get out.'

It was hot and stuffy in his little private room, but Jessica had been to the nearby shops again and bought him a carton of beer, a bottle of wine, cheese, ham, a baguette and a small plastic fan.

I eyed off his bottle of wine. 'If the doctors are happy with the operation that is an excellent sign,' I said. 'And hospital food is always crap. Look at the lovely cheese and ham Jessica has for you. Can I have a glass of your wine?'

Amanda encouraged him. 'You have the best health care in the world here,' she assured him and we certainly had no complaints about the lightning speed with which he had been picked up by the *pompiers*, been assessed at the hospital, taken into surgery and given a small but private room. There is no question his situation was miserable but one thing was evident: if you are going to have an accident, best do it in France.

18

A Lesson in Livers

We are on countdown to the end of the tour and there is talk of packing, of cramming new purchases into already overloaded suitcases, talk of meeting new itineraries for the next few weeks, talk of returning home to Australia.

It fills me with melancholy. The time has scampered by in a flurry of activity and excitement mixed with a touch of drama. Geoffrey, Amanda and I all have our own thoughts of how this tour has gone.

Amanda had envisioned this venture to be a cooking school; I had seen it more as a language and writer's retreat. Geoffrey, who had obviously quietly worried about the driving aspect, had visions of it being mostly about touring. It has turned out to be none of those things really, more a gathering of friends to celebrate the good life in the French countryside. The writing element hasn't really grabbed any of them; Eve and Ted were the only ones who even attempted to put pen to paper, but that doesn't matter at all. The cooking element has been more about eating than cooking. However, every meal has been memorable and we have all gleaned something significant from each of our demonstrating chefs. We have recipes for every dish we have eaten so in theory we can go home and cook French food with the confidence of the person who has been to France, bought its produce at the markets and watched it being cooked. Tomorrow there will be hands-on work when our guests all prepare a special dish for a farewell party. They are going to have free run of the kitchen to cook or create whatever they like.

The French lessons, so comprehensively given by Maurice, have not had a great deal of effect. Rosa has been the star pupil, but no-one else seems to have grasped more than the most basic of French words.

There are omissions on this tour that I can see now, small activities we should have undertaken. Perhaps we should have given the group more walks around the village, actually taken them to a lavender field or given them a roam around the surrounding vineyards and orchards. Several of them have taken morning walks by themselves or in pairs, mostly to combat the excesses of the night before. They have come back, puffed and glowing with pleasure at the charm of the preserved village.

'The village is so shut down from the outside you wouldn't know anyone lived here,' Sharon said yesterday when she and Margaret returned from an hour's tramp. 'Because the doors and windows on all the homes are shut, you would have no idea there was any activity going on, yet if you are lucky enough to come across an open door or a low stone fence where you can see into the interior or the back of the house, you realise there is a whole lot of living happening.'

She's right. Walk around the narrow village streets and St. Maximin appears lifeless. The front doors of properties lead right off the narrow roads; the stone-walled exteriors of the homes with small closed and shuttered windows give no indication of any life inside. Indeed, next door at Hester's Ab Fab apartments, the walls and doors are so formidable the place appears to be an abandoned fortress. Yet once through those giant wooden gates, you are in a little haven of French charm. St. Maximin is enchanting and I wished I had been able to get out for more walks to explore it. From my small window in the bunk room, I can see into back areas of the properties across the road, into fascinating stone-walled gardens crammed with overflowing flower pots. It couldn't be more French.

While the guests have been out taking early-morning walks, Amanda, Geoffrey and I have had morning meetings as Leith had directed. Geoffrey has led the discussion, pointing out any mistakes we might have made the previous day, looking at areas where we could improve our performance as tour leaders, carefully analysing all aspects of the services we provide for the guests. His calm manner and constant reassurance is priceless. He has been meticulous about financial records, writing out every item of expenditure right down to a euro or two on extra baguettes. When

I am not at the laptop in the kitchen, he is, poring over his financial spreadsheet with fierce concentration. Amanda is completely trusting in him, as indeed, am I. He could be fiddling the books for all we knew or cared. Neither of us is of a nature to fret over such mundane matters as to how financially viable this tour is; we do not have the personalities to concern ourselves about whether we are losing money or covering our expenses. We have never once thought about petrol costs, chefs' fees, entry prices to attractions, market purchases or restaurant bills. Geoffrey has taken care of all bills. He attempted on one or two fruitless occasions to get us to look at his spreadsheet but we were unable to concentrate on the boring figures for more than a minute.

I think Geoffrey, Amanda and I make a good tour trio: Amanda with her flirtatious and vibrant personality charming all the guests, not to mention her vital connections in France that have enabled us to experience local culture so close-up and personal; me with my genuine concern for the welfare and happiness of all our guests; Geoffrey with his indispensable help in every aspect, from driving us safely to ensuring our wine supplies never run out. The filming has gone very well, although we have not looked at any of the rushes ... (I like saying that, it's very movie-speak). Amanda doesn't seem as passionate any more about her dream of becoming a television presenter. Like me, I think she has been swept away with the demanding job of looking after the guests. It hasn't left any time for extra-curricular activities. She has even curtailed her truck trysts. She did manage one more country truck assignation but she was very discreet; the guests did not even know she had quietly slipped away for a few hours. Her love life has been mostly confined to phone and email sex these past two weeks and I'm proud of her. That she would be distracted by her lovers during our tour had been a concern for me before we started, but she has behaved admirably.

Whether we have given our guests a cooking school, a writer's retreat or a language school doesn't really matter. Every one of our guests says they have enjoyed themselves as never before. The evidence is there every day in the way they greet each other, in the way they interact, in the way they are so obviously comfortable with Maison de Maîtresse and with us. I feel like a proud mother.

Tonight is to be perhaps the pinnacle among highlights. We are visiting the Château St. Maximin for a *foie gras* lesson. Amanda has told us a number of times that this is a rare privilege, and indeed, our treasurer Geoffrey, has had to take a whopping chunk out of our budget to pay for this class. In fact, the class is so expensive, Amanda, Geoffrey and I cannot participate; our budget would not stretch to the purchase of three more duck livers. We must sit at the back of the class and watch the others at work.

'We'll take a bottle of wine and drink while they work,' Amanda said, to which I told her she was a genius. The Chateau is owned by a flamboyant gay couple, Jean-Marc Perry and Alain Manière. Alain's father, Jacques Manière was a famous French chef who invented the method of cooking in vapour and was much celebrated in French culinary circles. I met Alain and Jean-Marc last year. They have turned a twelfth-century chateau into one of the country's most elegant *chambre d'hôtes*. They take in only a few privileged guests at a time who enjoy a stay of indulgence and hedonism. They had agreed to open the chateau tonight especially for our group. This honour was, of course, due to their affection for Amanda. She has spent many party nights at the chateau, the most recent a Priscilla party where she donned a purple wig, painted her lips a vivid red, climbed into her sluttiest outfit and glued on false eyelashes so long they reached the middle of her forehead. Along with a bunch of locals dressed up in a similar garish manner, she partied at the chateau until five in the morning. As I have indicated, there is much colourful life going on behind St. Maximin's closed doors and shuttered windows.

Jean-Marc and Alain make an interesting couple. Like Johnny and Michel, they have been together a long time, although they are not married. Jean-Marc is outrageously handsome with strong white teeth and razor-sharp cheek bones, tall with wide shoulders and a flat stomach. His French charm melts everyone who comes into his space: men, women, children, even dogs. His English is perfect, his accent sexy, his clothes designer label. 'What a waste,' the ladies all murmured when he greeted them at the grand doors of the chateau with three-cheek kisses and a soft '*bonsoir*'. Rosa, her designer-label eye trained to spot a luxury brand from a distance equal to that of Earth to Mars, instantly took in the cut of his immaculate jeans and the European style of his lemon-and-black striped sweater.

Alain, while obviously not interested in designer labels and having no English, is the shy part of the duo, happy to let Jean-Marc take the limelight. Alain was to give us our *foie gras* lesson while Jean-Marc translated. But first, we were to experience the chateau grounds.

Château St. Maximin fulfils any fantasy you may have had about a French castle. And if you have never had such a fantasy then let me offer you one. Its romance and sense of unashamed luxury is evident right at the front iron gates. Press a button and Jean-Marc's mellifluous voice welcomes you while the large gates open silently and smoothly to reveal an enormous plant-filled, pebbled courtyard. The small pebbles crunch underfoot as you take in the orderly gardens. It is so peaceful even the sweet song of a small bird seems to have been deliberately staged to meld with the gentle trickling of a water fountain. Through the large front doors into the spacious foyer filled with antique furniture, the eye is led through a vast stone archway to a large courtyard flanked on three sides by the imposing stone walls of the chateau. It's almost dizzying in its grandeur.

With Jean-Marc and his little bouncing dog we gathered in the courtyard by a handsome circular fountain. Here cypress trees were clipped to perfect points, small hedges were coiffured to form neat round balls, paths were swept of any errant leaves, and flowerbeds flourished. There was a sense of calm and equilibrium, a feeling of order and grace. An oblong swimming pool built up on a level just below the mezzanine overlooked the gardens, guarded by bronze statues in provocative poses. Up a stately stone stairway leading off the mezzanine level, Jean-Marc and Alain have created another lush garden. A gnarled and twisted olive tree with an unmistakable air of ancient beauty lorded over the low shrubs and myriad herbs.

Our cameras clicked constantly as we strolled along a paved pathway with poppies and lavender bushes brushing our ankles. Amanda, a regular visitor to the chateau, took on the role of *chatelaine*, the lady of the manor, and led us around the gardens pointing out highlights, naming herbs and plants, offering an invitation to smell a rose, giving us little snippets of history.

Everyone had dressed up for the occasion. Rosa's slim body was wrapped in a black halter dress; Sharon looked fresh in neck-to-knee white skirt and top, Amanda looked suitably outrageous in a black see-through blouse loaded down with extravagant jewellery. Even Geoffrey had donned his best black shirt and pants and looked Godfather-like as he wandered around the gardens. Gino, who had by now shed his cloak of shyness, had taken over the role of camera assistant to Jessica in Leith's absence and helped her with the boom microphone and fussed over camera cases.

Inside, stone archways and alcoved windows served as a backdrop to antique furniture pieces. Elaborate candelabra, gilt framed mirrors, a stag's head above the large stone fireplace all spoke of good taste and a sense of style. I could have swept Amanda up in a great hug for giving us the opportunity to visit this splendid chateau. She flirted outrageously (but ineffectually) with Jean-Marc, kissed Alain and chatted to them both in her excellent French. After we had taken a little tour of the elegant living areas, Jean-Marc ordered his little bouncing dog outside and asked everyone to remove their rings, go to the washroom, thoroughly wash their hands and then don plastic gloves. Everyone looked perplexed.

'We are going to remove the nerve from the livers,' Jean-Marc translated for Alain. 'We must be scrupulously clean.' After much shuffling, hand-washing and ring removal, everyone was seated at a handsome polished table in the large dining room with an enormous pale pink liver quivering in front of them.

Touching a liver is unpleasant to many people, removing a nerve from one is particularly abhorrent. I encouraged everyone. 'You'll love it,' I gushed. 'No other tour in all of France offers this rare experience. Removing a nerve from a fat pink liver is fun; everybody knows that.' They grimaced and ignored me.

Alain had overestimated his liver purchases and there was one spare. It was offered to Geoffrey, who took his place nervously at the table with the others.

Let us pause for a moment to consider *foie gras. Foie gras* translates, as you surely know because you are a discerning reader—you must be, you are reading this book—as 'fat liver'. *Foie gras* is up there in the luxury gastronomic stakes with Beluga caviar and black truffles. The duck or goose liver is obscenely engorged after the birds spend their short lives being force fed enormous quantities of corn. It is a controversial product, because let's be frank, no-one wants to think about an adorable duck or a cute goose having a great big funnel shoved down its neck and a sack of corn poured down it. However, I doubt the gourmands of the world ever think about the discomfort of a duck or a goose as they spread their rich, smooth *foie gras* on a slice of Melba toast. And it is best we don't either. Best to think of ducks and geese in the cute, cartoon-like way they are portrayed on signs at the front of small *foie gras* farms in rural France—happy, adorable and dancing with their beaks open in big smiles. France is not the only country producing this luxury product. Israel and Madagascar also produce the fat livers, and Alain said he had never seen such large livers as he had in Chicago.

'Never had I come across such big livers before,' he said through Jean-Marc's translation. 'But now it is forbidden to eat *foie gras* in Chicago.'

I think he meant the manufacture is outlawed in Chicago, as I can't imagine rich, chubby Americans being told they were forbidden to eat anything.

Jean-Marc addressed the group. 'Has anyone made *foie gras* before?' he asked in his sexy accent.

This brought on amused looks. These were true-blue Aussies. None of them had probably even eaten a meal of liver and bacon before, let alone knew how *foie gras* was made.

'Isn't this fun?' I called from the back of the room and then joined Amanda in opening our bottle of rosé wine.

The guests were all troupers. With the back of a small spoon and with their faces screwed up tightly, they proceeded to remove the nerves from the enormous livers.

'*Foie gras* originates from Egypt,' Alain told them as they worked on the livers. 'It was made as far back as the time of the Pharaohs. The Egyptians used to stuff geese with figs to make the livers bigger. When you buy a liver now, it must be a consistent colour. If the surface has little spots or tiny splotches of blood on it, do not buy it.'

I doubt anyone in the room would ever consider looking at a liver at the market let alone examining it for little spots or splotches of blood. But it was interesting to learn liver purchasing techniques.

The reason for the nerve removal is to ensure the liver has a consistent smooth, butter-like texture. There are two main nerves in the liver. They are hard, and it would kill the pleasure of eating a luxurious product were you to encounter one as you ate. After the nerves are removed, the liver is pressed back into shape and then pushed down into jars for preserving.

At least that is the theory, but our dear guests, alarmed before these large pink blobs, managed to make a mess of their livers. 'You must be gentle with the liver,' cried Alain 'You must not be brutal. It is a very fragile thing. If you are brutal with it, it will not cook properly. You must respect the liver.' He paced around the table watching everyone with a pained expression.

This simple process of nerve removal required the delicate touch of a skilled micro-surgeon and not one of our group was up to the job. When they had finally removed the loathsome nerves, each person was left with a yellowish, pinky mass resembling something so vile I won't mention it because I want you to forever think of *foie gras* as the luxury product it is. Dear Geoffrey had managed to make the biggest mess of all. His liver resembled a pile of pale pink mincemeat but Alain and Jean-Marc were polite and tried to hide their alarmed expressions. After seasoning the livers, they helped everyone get their liver mess into the sterilising jars, leaving room at the top to pour a liberal amount of sweet white wine over it to counteract the richness of the liver. The jars were then going to sit overnight before Alain would put them into a water bath tomorrow for the final step, the preserving.

'The jars must be under the water the whole time,' Alain said. 'They will be kept in the boiling water for 35 minutes. The water must be bubbling, not just simmering. It is very important the jar is under the water so it is really sterilised.'

By this time, Amanda and I, sitting at the back of the room had consumed almost a bottle of rosé between us. As the guests removed their rubber gloves dripping with bits of wiggly nerve endings and pink liver debris, and tried to compose their expressions back to serenity once more, Amanda shouted. 'Wasn't that fabulous?' I took another sip of wine and roared. 'What a wonderful experience'

We deserved their scorn, but they all looked at us happily, much in the manner a child does when he knows his mother is misbehaving and he is much smarter than her.

After Alain had taken the jars out to his kitchen, he produced a log of *foie gras* he had made for our tasting, its smooth surface runny with yellow fat. With much flourish and several shouts of *voilà* he dipped a sharp knife in warm water and with all the respect and concentration of a cosmetic surgeon about to give

Angelina Jolie an unnecessary face lift, he sliced cleanly through its sumptuousness. He served it with chunks of baguette and homemade fig and rhubarb chutneys. He poured glasses of sweet wine for everyone.

'You should always serve the *foie gras* with a sweet wine to counteract the richness,' he said. 'Champagne also works well. The bubbles balance the fattiness. The chutneys work well with *foie gras* but so does fresh fruit, or apple slices sautéed in a little butter.'

This part Amanda and I could join in, and all I am going to say is this: bite into a mouthful of smooth, rich *foie gras* topped with a *soupçon* of fruity chutney and then take a sip of the sweet wine and you will not only make little whimpering noises of the orgasmic kind, you will be taken on a brief holiday to Eden. Then as you reach for another slice, you will determine, like the French wisely do, never to allow your mind to dwell for a moment on a duck, a goose, a funnel or a bag of corn.

We walked the few metres back to Maison de Maîtresse in the dark silence of St. Maximin, the clopping of our feet on the cobbled paths the only sound in the sleeping village. We passed the small stone community hall. The lights were on and inside a beautiful slim young man was dancing by himself. He appeared completely lost in the rap music coming from a small cassette player, his feet and arms moving at lightning speed with complicated movements. He was obviously rehearsing at competition level; he danced better than Michael Jackson. We all stopped and watched him through the window. It was such an incongruous sight—the modern dance, the old building, the near-silent village—we all piled inside and began loudly clapping him. He stopped dancing and laughed. We pleaded with him to dance again and although he had no English, he understood us immediately. He put on the rap music and gave us a private performance so virtuoso we were all speechless. Then we began to dance with him. We rapped, we twirled, we moonwalked. Joan and I got clumsily down on the floor and with our arms and legs in the air attempted a rap twirl on our bums. The young man did not laugh at us, did not even snigger at the two old ladies rap dancing in a community hall in a rural village in France. The contrast with where we had just come from was so vast, it made us love St. Maximin all the more.

19

Au Revoir but Never Adieu

$\mathcal{G}$eoffrey and I have moved into a two-bedroom apartment at Ab Fab. Oh, the joy of it, the sheer bloody happiness of it. A bed. A double one. Up off the floor. No more trying to heave myself up off the mattress every morning like a lumbering hippopotamus struggling out of a mud hole. No more aching back and bad morning temper. No more lying on the hall landing with my head hanging in the bathroom trying to find the plug for the hair dryer. It may be for just two nights, but two nights at Ab Fab will be two nights of bed heaven.

The move came as a surprise. Amanda suddenly realised yesterday, that Ab Fab was empty now that Maurice, Françoise, Luce, Rosemary, Michel or any other of our visiting chefs would no longer require accommodation. And Ciara did not need to be housed any more since we sacked her. The poor girl had had the courage to come to Maison de Maîtresse the day after her drunken appearance and apologise to everyone.

'I'm so sorry for my awful behaviour,' she said in her Irish lilt and everyone instantly forgave her. We should have known such a person would not be content washing dishes and waiting tables; she is the sort of person who must be the centre of attention at all times. As she left, I hugged her, and to my surprise she offered her services for future work, this time as a documentary producer.

'If you want me to make a film for you, I've plenty of experience,' she said. 'I could assist Jessica and Leith and yourself in any future projects.'

'Er … haven't we just fired you from one project,' I said quietly. 'Why would we take you on for another?'

She missed what I said entirely and talked on happily about her experience as a movie-maker as she packed her bag to leave. I had nothing but admiration for her.

Ab Fab is a sanctuary of serenity after the bustle next door. I can roam around the apartment, lie on all the beds, sit out on the balcony and look for miles at the neat patchwork quilt of French countryside. I can linger for a morning lie-in in the bedroom overlooking the courtyard and beyond, where somebody in the village keeps chickens and a rooster. Although having just written that sentence, I realise the words 'lie in' and 'rooster' do not exactly go together. But what do I care? Let the rooster crow his little knackers off. I have a two-bedroom apartment to share with Geoffrey. Ab Fab is only a few steps away from the group so I am hardly abandoning my guests on this, our last day of the tour.

This morning Amanda and I pottered around her garden while Geoffrey took the guests supermarket shopping. Piers arrived with his extensive DJ equipment including two enormous speakers which had me worrying.

'What will the cretins do?' I asked Amanda.

'Their usual cretin stuff,' she said dismissively, although she did look a little worried. She did not want the *gendarme* called once again. She was torn between her duty to the community and her desire to throw a good party. The party desire won over, of course. She had invited all the chefs and their entourages who had helped us over the past two weeks and as usual, she had no idea how many people would actually turn up. It could be 10, it could be 50.

'We will just throw another sausage on the barbecue,' she said, when I expressed concern at the uncertainty of the party numbers.

'Another sausage won't feed 20 more people if that many turn up,' I argued, but nothing could dampen her fickle spirit. 'Then I will just open a few cans of *canard*,' she said. 'You can never go short when you have cans of *canard* in the cupboard.'

Amanda has many cans of *canard* on her stairwell shelves. *Canard* is the French word for duck; good-sized pieces of crispy skinned duck cooked in fat can be purchased in cans at the markets and supermarkets. Just open the can, gently heat the duck pieces, toss a green salad and maybe boil a few small potatoes, and you have a delicious meal of restaurant quality on the table in a very short time. It's delicious and a speedy way to serve duck.

Our group arrived back with their baskets loaded with groceries and produce and took over the kitchen.

Ted had wisely stayed home this morning and made a *pissaladière* from the recipe he learnt at Dean's cooking demonstration. He had quietly gone about his baking while the others were out shopping and his tart was ready to be reheated tonight. Eve made a refreshing salad of watermelon and chopped mint. Shirley made a raw mushroom salad, slicing mushrooms with all the speed of a restaurant chef.

Rosa took a platter of sliced zucchinis out to the barbecue and began chargrilling them. 'I'll make a dressing of garlic, mint and balsamic,' she said, turning them over on the barbecue so they showed the lovely brown stripes of the grill.

Sharon cut thick slices off large eggplants and halved red and yellow peppers. 'I am going to do a simple plate of chargrilled vegetables,' she said. 'I'll roast the capsicum until they blacken and give off a lovely smoked flavour. Then I'll peel them and puree them into a kind of red pepper pesto.'

It was all going very well and the guests were obviously enjoying cooking. Not one of them seemed to have a problem with the oven.

I left them to return to Ab Fab where I bounced on the bed in the main bedroom, sat on the twin beds in the second bedroom, sat on the balcony admiring the country view for a short while before going back down to the bedroom to bounce on the bed again.

I felt elated and happy, sad and melancholy.

I have to be honest and say I was glad the tour was over. The responsibility of looking after people, the worrying over their happiness and the fear for their safety had played havoc with my wellbeing. We had shared an unforgettable 14 days together and, thank God—oh really thank you God, thank you so much —nothing awful had happened to any of them, even if we'd had our own bit of rotten luck.

Leith was still miserable in the hospital. He was frustrated, angry, and uncomfortable and now hated France and all French people.

I felt personally responsible for his broken leg and overall discomfort. If it wasn't for me he would not have been in a stuffy hospital room in France; he would have been home in Cairns in Queensland, running his diving business, diving in the coral-filled waters of the Great Barrier Reef, taking photos of colourful fish and spectacular coral formations.

The Australian insurance company had been wonderful and this was some comfort, but my guilt was corrosive. If it wasn't for Geoffrey's gentle insistence that we must carry on as normal, I would have stayed with them until their arrangements to get home were in place.

The party began with just us. I wanted to make a speech to our guests. We assembled by the pool.

I told them how much I appreciated them, then went through the group one by one, pointing out their highlights and their contribution to the tour. I meant everything I said. I thanked Amanda and Geoffrey. Amanda made a speech and said more good words before shaking her boobs at every one. Then we all gushed at one another and said how much we loved each other, and then, feeling exhausted from all this bonhomie, we sat down and out came the Beaujolais soup.

Sasha and her husband arrived. John New Zealand came. Hester came in with two newly arrived Ab Fab guests and a plate of stuffed eggs. Jean-Marc arrived with our jars of *foie gras* and everyone swooned at his loveliness. Piers cranked up the music. We danced. Amanda and Margaret got Gino in a sandwich situation and Amanda rubbed herself up and down his back. He looked terrified. Then Amanda danced by herself and lifted up her dress to show us her bare brown buttocks. There might have been a g-string there, but if there was it was lost in the deep valley between those lovely plump buns. I watched her dancing with complete abandon, lifting her skirt like a Spanish flamenco dancer, singing to the music, tossing her big blonde hair and laughing joyfully up to the early evening sky, and I thought: I want to be her. Amanda is always happy, she embraces life and all that it throws at her. She needs no permanent man to make her life full and happy. She can be the consummate hostess, the outrageous flirt, the ultimate party girl, the chef, the cook, the cleaner, the organiser. She can be anything she wants to be, and she is everything she wants to be. She once told me if I ever, God forbid, found myself without Geoffrey (and only death will part us) that I should never look for fulfilment from a man.

'Don't just hook up with a man because you are on your own,' she said. 'No woman should do that, no matter her age. Make yourself happy.'

I left the party after we had eaten, hoping to escape to Ab Fab only for a quick rest. I was exhausted and not up to dancing—maybe it was all that twirling on my backside on the community hall floor last night. I took the enormous jailor's key to the Ab Fab gates and quietly snuck away. I had been lying on the bed for only ten minutes when Jessica banged on the door, trying to get me back to the party. I let her in with the big key, gave it to her to go back to the party and told her to come and sleep in the spare bedroom when she was ready. She had been sleeping on a mattress floor in the living room, remember? She locked me in and took the key.

After half an hour I felt refreshed and ready to go back to the party. I pulled on my versatile black dress again, in a strapless look this time, and got ready to return to Maison de Maîtresse. I couldn't get out. The big door could only be opened from the inside with the key I had given Jessica. I tried another escape through a door that led to Hester's private apartment. That too was locked. I could hear the music thumping behind the walls of Amanda's garden and I called out the window. No-one came. I lay back on the bed and fretted for an hour. Then I fell asleep and awoke in the grey light of dawn to the rooster's crowing. There was no sign of Geoffrey or Jessica. I stuck my head out the window again but was too nervous to call out in case the entire neighbourhood, apart from Jessica and Geoffrey, was asleep. I waited and fretted. The rooster crowed into the dawn. I dozed off again, during which time Jessica had come back and slumped on the bed in the spare room in the kind of deep sleep a person who has partied until dawn enjoys. I tried to rouse her, to find out where the key was, but I couldn't move her. I have never felt so trapped.

I waited for another hour and then tried to rouse Jessica again. I did manage to wake her whereupon I immediately asked her where her father and the key were, but she just mumbled incoherently. By now the sun was out, the rooster was still crowing and I could hear Hester's new guests enjoying breakfast in the courtyard. I thought of calling them to come and help me, but decided an old lady locked in the house would look stupid. I roused Jessica once more and this time managed to find out where the key was. I had no watch, no clock, no idea what time of day it was. When I finally let myself out of Ab Fab I raced the few steps to Maison de Maîtresse to find I had no key to get in. I bashed so loudly on the door all of the inhabitants of St. Maximin could have come to my assistance had they so cared. At last Shirley came to the door and I fell in. Geoffrey was sitting in the kitchen of the small house eating croissants with several of the ladies.

'Good morning,' he said brightly.

'Where were you all night?' I said, not so brightly. 'I've been worried sick and trapped in Ab Fab.'

He didn't want to admit it in front of the ladies but he had slept all night over the laptop in the kitchen of the big house where he had gone to make some last-minute financial entries. This is not as odd as it sounds. At home in Australia after an evening involving a larger than normal quantity of alcohol, Geoffrey has been known to sleep the night away quite happily at his computer; he sometimes sleeps all night sitting upright on a kitchen stool snoring robustly until dawn.

Now, after two weeks of sleeping on a narrow small bunk bed, when he had the opportunity to enjoy a comfortable night's sleep in a big bed at Ab Fab, he had chosen instead to sleep sitting upright in a kitchen chair.

But he looked refreshed.

Maybe he had really spent the night in Amanda's bed.

We helped the guests with their heavy suitcases and even heavier hearts. Geoffrey was to drive them to Avignon.

I gave each guest a hug, told them they were the best group a travel God could ever have sent to a novice tour leader and then they all piled into the van. Geoffrey started the van and for the first time since the beginning of the tour, he managed the cranky brake without a single jerk. He took off smoothly and drove them out of St. Maximin and my life.

Later in the afternoon, as Amanda, Geoffrey, Jessica and I sat with a glass of wine in the walled garden, the property seemed empty and lonely.

'We're going to Greece tomorrow,' Amanda said suddenly and made a whooping sound of excitement. Like me, she felt free of all responsibility now, but unlike me, she was happy and ready for a Greek holiday. I was beset by heartache at abandoning Jessica. Jessica was due to leave St. Maximin early this evening. A taxi had been arranged to take her to Arles where she would find a hotel near the hospital. She had no idea when or how she would get back to Australia. I wanted to weep into my glass of wine at the thought of her in France on her own. So I did.

There was surprise from Amanda and consternation from Jessica.

'I'll be fine, really I will,' Jessica said to cheer me up, but I was inconsolable by now and continued quietly weeping for the rest of the afternoon.

We stayed in the garden until the light began to fade and Jessica's taxi arrived. We went out to the little square to help her into the taxi and she reassured me over and over that she was fine. As the taxi rounded the tight corner out of the square, the church bells chimed and she stuck her arm out of the window and gave a cheery wave.

That night, Amanda, Geoffrey and I were alone for the first time in two weeks and we talked about the tour, the guests, the good times, the frustrating times: Ted and his washing machine fixation, Rosa and the turmoil of Gino's arrival, the ease with which

Joan had embraced all activities, the fun Margaret and Sharon had, the bond they had all formed. We marvelled at how Eve, whose husband had walked out on her so suddenly, had blossomed from Amanda's example and resolved that she had no need of a man to continue her life fully and happily

We talked about Les Baux-de-Provence, the icy wind the day of our Roussillon trip, the kayaking to the spectacular Pont du Gard. We talked about food: the rich *coq au vin,* the little frogs' legs, the delicate soufflé, the drunken quail, the awful flaming bananas. We talked about Maurice and Françoise, about Michel and Christian and Rosemary and Alain and Jean-Marc. We talked about ourselves, how proud we were that our guests all had such an unforgettable time. In between talking we lapsed into thoughtful silence.

After a while Amanda perked up. 'Would you be prepared to do it all again next year?' she asked me suddenly.

I thought about it for a few moments; about the unnecessary worry, my high stress levels, the discomfort of sleeping on the floor, those awful fantasies of death and organ stealing. I looked at her. *'Je voudrais absolument',* I replied … which loosely translates as: 'bloody oath, I would.'

Postscript

*I*n case I've left you wondering, here's an update.

Jessica found a hotel in Arles while Leith remained in hospital for about ten days. She took him out every day in a wheelchair down to a nearby lake where they fed ducks, drank wine (hospital staff always seemed to have a wine opener in their pockets) and watched sunsets. She said it was all really rather pleasant and neither of them felt as though they missed out on Greece. Their insurance company flew them both first-class back to Australia where they immediately immersed themselves back in their business. The Australian doctors were very impressed with the neatness of the French surgeons' work and Leith has healed perfectly.

Amanda, Geoffrey and I went to Mykonos for a week where we rested and played with fabulous gay men and drank a lot of cocktails. Amanda was in her element on the nudist beaches and at the nightclubs.

Rosa and Gino are together and happier than ever according to a last email message from her. All of our guests have continued contact with each other since the tour.

Geoffrey spent hundreds of hours editing the extensive filming, often sitting up all night at the computer, where he drifted off into a comfortable sleep around two in the morning. He taught himself all the intricacies of film editing and became quite the Steven Spielberg. Then his hard drive crashed and he lost the lot. He swore, I swore. He fumed, I fumed. Then he started the whole process over again from the original film cassettes. He is still toiling away on the project (and sleeping very well at the computer).

Amanda has had some dramatic developments with *Chocolat* involving midnight spying missions to Morocco and recovery of certain monies. Two new potential lovers have been added to her growing list ... a Sean Connery lookalike (in his younger days) and another dashing Moroccan. You will have to wait for a follow-up book for more juicy details.

Geoffrey, Amanda and I have just completed another successful two-week tour of Provence with Maison de Maîtresse as our base, along with all our dear French friends and visiting chefs. Go to my website www.annrickard.com and take a look at us partying in Provence. We have called our tours Ooh La La ... Provence and Beyond, and plan to extend our tours in future to take in Greece, Italy and ... maybe Morocco. Why not come and join us?

Ann Rickard

About Ann Rickard

In her own words, Ann Rickard is an 'old Aussie sheila" who burst onto the travel writing scene late in life when her humorous travel narratives won her a legion of fans.

Her first book, *Not Another Book About Italy*, was an instant success. Excerpts from her follow-up book, *Not Another Greek Salad*, won her the ASTW Travel Writer of the Year Award in 2005. Her third book, *The Last Book About Italy*, continued her Italy stories and her fourth book, *Flash and Brash with Fries on the Side*, won the title of ASTW Travel Book of the Year for 2007.

As well as writing books and travelling, Ann works full-time as a lifestyle editor for the *Noosa News* on Queensland's Sunshine Coast. She also writes a humorous weekly column entitled 'Old Wives' Tales' in *The Sunshine Coast Daily*.

Ann's latest goal is to spend a large part of her year in France and the rest at her home in Noosa where she admits to living an enviable lifestyle with her devoted husband, Geoffrey, and two little dogs, LuLu and Cossie.

www.annrickard.com

Amanda and Ann with a New Orleans Jazz man

Amanda's table